Spike Milligan has written novels, poems, children's stories, TV shows and countless letters. Most of these have appeared in book form. In response to an overwhelming demand for more material for the avid Milligan reader, we present a collection of the articles he has written for various newspapers and periodicals. The inclusion of Scunthorpe is, quite simply, an inclusion of Scunthorpe, and should be taken in that spirit. Obviously you have to read the book to understand fully the irrelevance of its appearance.

Mrs Griselda Thrills's boarding house in Scunthorpe

Indefinite Articles
(Culled from his Newspaper Writings)
& SCUNTHORPE
Spike Milligan

SPHERE BOOKS LIMITED
30-32 Gray's Inn Road, London WC1X 8JL

First published in Great Britain by
Michael Joseph Ltd and M & J Hobbs 1981

Copyright © 1981 by Spike Milligan Productions

Published by Sphere Books Ltd 1983

Set in Times

Printed and bound in Great Britain by
Collins, Glasgow

Contents

Foreword

by Jack Hobbs

Spike Milligan is a lazy writer. In fact I find it very difficult to get him to write a book, so in desperation and in view of the fact that Christmas is coming and the geese are getting fat, but I'm not, I decided to go through his fridge in the hopes of sustenance and found the enclosed old articles in cold storage.

I have welded them, after defrosting, into a manuscript from which, with the aid of Scunthorpe, I have produced a book which has totally baffled Michael Joseph. They are so worried by it that they are thinking of changing their name to Albania.

The inclusion of Scunthorpe is an inclusion of Scunthorpe and lifts the book into an area yet to be discovered, but no doubt some of you will find it, booksellers and W. H. Smith's willing.

I think it's a funny book and an ideal gift for any lunatic in the family, and let's face it every family's got them. What do you think? Answers personally to me on the back of a twenty-pound note.

Note: We would like the people of Scunthorpe to know that the references to Scunthorpe are nothing personal. It is a JOKE, as is Scunthorpe.

Visitors enjoying the annual Scunthorpe floods

A Tribute to Scunthorpe

from William McGonagall

Ooh wonderful Scunthorpe town,
I can never think of you without a frown.
Oh I remember the wonderful treats
Of swimming in Scunthorpe's flooded streets.
And who can forget that gale force nine
Which removed all my nether garments
Off the washing-line?
And they've blown next door into Mrs Thrills's garden,
So I took them back with a 'I beg your pardon.'
She said, 'Come partake of my home-made beer.'
And so I was in hospital for over a year.
And when I told the doctor I'd dined with Mrs Thrills
He said, 'Then you're bloody lucky you're not buried
                                   up in those hills.'
Apart from that, I've always loved Scunthorpe.

signed
WILLIAM Mc GONAGALL 1883

A crowded beach at Scunthorpe
in the height of the season

Eccentrics

According to Cassell's three-page dictionary for computerized idiots, the word eccentric means: 'Deviating from the centre; an oddity; a mechanical contrivance for converting circular into reciprocating rectilinear motion, especially that operating the side valve of a steam engine'. Having been accused by the Boulting Brothers of being an eccentric, I am puzzled as to why they didn't give me my correct title, i.e. a mechanical contrivance for converting circular into reciprocating etc. etc. etc. . .

So . . . when Willy Davis said, 'Milligan, kneel down, I the God of *Punch* dub thee Writer, go, write something about Eccentrics,' I began to wonder just why I was one and had never noticed it. I mean, when I read Oliver St John Gogarty's description of a gentleman waiting to cross Sackville Street dressed in a top hat, a football jersey, evening dress jacket, cricket pads, a girdled cavalry sword and holding a red guard's van flag, I thought *that* was an eccentric – but no, apparently nobody even noticed him, so who were the eccentrics – him, or the passing pedestrians? It's difficult to say; however, racing back through my boyhood I realized that my whole family were, as I said, mechanical contrivances for converting circular into etc. etc. . .

Let's start with my father. For a start I thought every football fan who listened to his team (Arsenal) on the wireless, like my father wore a red and white football jersey, and carried a football rattle and took swigs from a beer bottle. When TV started and he could see the game, he added a referee's whistle. Even on that he had a variant; he would turn off the TV sound, blindfold himself and listen to the radio commentary, every now and then stealing a

1

glance at the screen to see if the commentary tied up with the game.

The night before the match he would unroll a small plan of a football pitch, and, using sugar lumps dipped in red ink for Arsenal, he would lock himself in the parlour. We could hear him shouting out instructions. 'It's the long ball down the middle that will do it . . . forget flank penetration, there's too many in the goalmouth, it's the headed ball *over* the defence . . . 3 goals and you're onto a bonus of 10 shillings a man . . . you can live it up . . .' and so on. For economy's sake my mother had to use the inked sugar cubes, and all through the soccer season I drank red tea.

My mother's side, the Kettlebands, were also mechanical contrivances etc., especially my late Uncle Hughie, who would try and see how far he could walk without opening his eyes. He once managed three-quarters of a mile. For this he chose a large, barren, treeless plain in Hyderabadsind, but it took him so long he was stricken with sunstroke. He moved to London where there were no large treeless plains; trying to break his record he was knocked down by a tram in Catford, SE6. When he was discharged from Lewisham Hospital, he took up another test of self control, holding his breath underwater. He calculated the less pressure on the body the less exertion and therefore a longer duration of breath retention, so he would lie on his bed face down, his head hanging over the foot of the bed. He also believed that cold water absorbed body energy (true), consequently the water had to be at body temperature, 98.4 degrees. So that he could time it to perfection, he bought a waterproof stop-watch that he placed at the bottom of the bucket; this was so that no time was lost in having to take head from water to look at stop-watch. He managed up to two minutes but this brought on nose bleeds and terminated his attempts.

He then settled for seeing if it was possible to sleep in the upright position, and many's the night I awoke to see him standing on his bed at three in the morning. After two weeks he still hadn't managed it. He persisted and then one night, in the early hours, I heard a terrible THUD and a groan; he had fallen asleep, his legs had collapsed and he had been catapulted to the concrete floor which split his head open. 'Must have lost control,' he said as we bandaged his head.

2

This, dear reader, is not all. His mother, the late Margaret Burnside-Kettleband (my grandmother), who looked the epitome of normality, left behind her a trail of yellow powder. She swore she had never had arthritis in her legs because every morning she poured two ounces of sulphur into her socks. When she and grandpa did the Lancers at the gallop at the Governor's Ball (Poona) they were soon swirling in a knee-high yellow dust. My grandpa, Trumpet-majôr Alfred Henry Kettleband MM, was all in the same mould.

A respectable, rich Hindu lad, one Percy Lalkaka (Urdu translation: 'Red Dung') fell madly in love with my Auntie Eileen, but he was frightened off. My grandfather would frequently appear in his wife's floral nightgown. Holding a boiled egg in a spoon, he would glide past them, grinning and saying. 'There's going to be frost tonight in Quetta,' and disappear into the bathroom where he could be heard pouring buckets of water into the WD bath. A pause, then he would reappear, clad in shorts, now holding a spoonful of curry powder: 'But . . . it's going to be damned hot to-night.' It terminated the romance.

All that I have told you I accepted as normal. I was five at the time. I became personally involved in eccentricity (that's off-peak electricity), when my father, owing to his strange behaviour in India, was posted to Rangoon as a Sergeant in the Port Defence. One day he came to me. 'Son,' he said, 'The jungles are full of Dacoits, you must learn to defend yourself, come with me.' He placed me behind a rock and gave me an old Lee-Enfield filled with blanks, while he, wearing a dragon mask, plunged into the undergrowth. 'When you see me, fire, and I will judge if you have scored a hit.' As he ran hither and thither I blazed away. Occasionally he would shout, 'A hit, a hit,' and then stick a red adhesive spot on his body or face.

Came three o'clock, he was a mass of red spots and exhausted, but worse was to come. A nursing mother kite-hawk (wing span five feet) dove on him and clawed off his wig and flew away. It was a puzzled coolie who saw a man covered in red spots, with a bald and bleeding head, shouting up at the sky and throwing rocks in the air. The next day my father decided not to be the target, so he got several puzzled coolies to surround him holding *lathis* (police

3

sticks) and, wielding two blank cartridge pistols, he blazed away, forcing the victims to stick on red spots when 'hit'.

Many of you may think that all I tell you is lies, but a picture was taken of the last incident. I leave you now to return to my life as a mechanical contrivance for converting circular etc. etc. Oh yes, the caption on the back of the photo, which is my father's own, reads, 'Picture taken in Burma in 1930 shows Captain Leo Milligan practising "Custer's Last Stand", which he learnt in New Mexico as a boy, using his own Lascars as the enemy and shooting soap bullets with a reduced charge.' Any questions?

A group photograph of some of the guests who have stayed at Mrs Thrills's boarding house

The Apology

The Apology is simple to explain: it is a device for avoiding crippling libel actions, as any *Private Eye* editor will gainsay. How many times have men who, in the heat of the moment, have been caught *in flagrante* with a business partner's wife, leapt from the bed and said to the husband: 'Jim, old boy, I'm sorry, now you know why I'm always late for board meetings.' It has never worked in this context, however. It gives the offender time to (a) work out an escape route, and (b) get his trousers before the litigation starts.

Basically the average Englishman, and most Englishmen are pretty average, is bursting to apologize. Spill soup on a diner's head and he will leap to his feet and say, 'I'm awfully sorry,' before flooring you. Some apologies are cover-ups, i.e. having hacked a cherry tree to death, and caught red-handed, Washington (the first in a long line of Richard Nixons) says: 'I cannot tell a lie, I did it.' Big deal!

I've made many apologies in my time. My most desperate one was in a pub, being seized upon by a drunken six-foot navvy, and it wasn't long before I was saying, 'I'm sorry for smashing my jaw to pieces on your innocent fist.'

An Australian life-guard rescued a hag of a woman from a raging sea. When he saw her face, he said to the husband: 'I'm sorry, mate, I didn't know.' Apologies are impossible to come by in car accidents. Never has a man extricated from the wreck of his Rolls Corniche said, 'Constable, it's all my fault. The 28 Scotsmen lying dead in the Mini Clubman are innocent.'

There are those devilish apologies that in fact are used to place the blame on the innocent parties (been to any innocent parties

5

lately, sailor?). It was in India, 1927. My grandfather was Sergeant in charge of military steamrollers. By some impossible circumstances he had killed, or rather ironed out, one Fusilier O'Brien. Grandfather was sent round to 'explain and apologize' to the widow.

'Good morning, madam. I'm sorry to say your husband has just died of deafness.'

'Deafness?'

'Yes, mam. There was this steamroller comin' up behind 'im and 'e didn't 'ear it comin'.'

It saved the government a lot of money, and Fusilier O'Brien was buried in an envelope. About this time, I remember, my father had to make an apology, and he took great care of the preparation. At bed-time he stood before a full-length mirror and struck a dramatic pose (struck any dramatic poses lately, sailor?).

'Dick, I've come to say I'm sorry.' He paced up and down. 'No! that's not good enough!' He struck a second pose. 'My dear Dick, I've been a cad, please forgive me.' Still dissatisfied, he knelt down, hung his head on his chest, and in an anguished, sobbing voice said: 'OOOOOOoooomy God, what have I done? Dick, Dick my dear and trusted friend, I've wronged you. I've been a swine. I'm not fit to kiss your boots.' I didn't understand. All he'd done was scratch the paint on Dick's bicycle, but my father believed an apology gave one tremendous dramatic scope, and my mother had to restrain him from pushing a hump up his back for the morrow.

An apology that really didn't have weight was when, after surrendering Singapore and his army of 180,000 to a Japanese Army of 40,000, General Percival wrote home:

> Dear Winston Churchill,
> I'm sorry.
> General Percival

Natives in the New Hebrides apologize by running their heads against their straw huts until they are demolished. The apologants wiped themselves out after the introduction of brick huts. This brings to the fore the apology alternatives: those who don't want to apologize can be given an apology task.

WIFE: 'What is Mr Sneddle next door doing cutting our lawn with nail scissors?'

HUSBAND: 'He chose it rather than say sorry for poisoning the cat.'

The whole world of the apology needs revision; it seems unfair that a boy who steals an apple and a man who has set fire to your house should both use the same word. No, there should be a graded scale. For a schoolboy, say, stealing a rubber: 'I'm sorry Junior Apology Grade A one.' And the variants, i.e.:

Tripping a pedestrian: 'I'm sorry Byeway Apology Grade 3 minimal.'

Hand on girl's knee in cinema: 'I'm sorry Kine-Apology Grade 8 Scale 23.'

Both hands on both girls' knees: As above plus 'Will you marry me?'

A woman receiving a note from a guest at her party might say: 'Dear Mrs DeVille; a lovely party and Socio-Apology Mictural-Botanical Grade 6 Scale 356/A', would mean: 'I'm sorry I widdled on your rose garden last night.'

And a GPO service for those who've never thrilled to an apology: 'Dial an Apology.' For a few pence an old spinster can hear a male voice say: 'Darling, I'm sorry I raped you last night', or a Jewish lady can hear an imitation of Hitler saying: 'I'm a Nazi swine, World War II was meiner fault.'

I'll conclude this brief piece with a story. A coloured musician was dying. His friend visited him and said, 'Man, I'm sorry you're dying.' The victim replied, '*You're* sorry?'

The Scunthorpe Hilton
(The wall is available to Arab visitors)

Gratitude

One day last week, whizz kid Silly Willy von Davis was fondling a 60-foot plaster cast of his overdraft, sipping after-shave lotion and partially out of his mind at the thought of the value added tax to come on his new lawn mower. He was toying with the idea of selling the sacred PUNCH LUNCH table whose engraved gravy stains by witless Victorian humorists would fetch a fortune in firewood. Suddenly he thought: SPIKE MILLIGAN! – yes, I'll commission that ashen-faced, ageing, 55-year-old Gael force seven to write some of his famous crapological writings (I think my sleeping outside his office door in rags did influence his decision).

Through the keyhole he says, 'Write 1,200 words on the word Gratitude. If you're stuck you can include Ingratitude as well.' BIG DEAL. It appears that Carl Foreman, a strolling film producer of no fixed cinema, and part-time baker (*The Buns of Navarone*, etc.) claimed that the word gratitude had enormous potential! No wonder this joker never got any higher than foreman. I look up the word in the dictionary, and there it is, 'twixt gratis and grattoir. Gratitude: *French* from the *Latin*, gratitudinem.

See? It's a bloody foreigner! Very well, we will start with them. Well, let's have a look at the Chinkee-Poos version of gratitude; Confucius say: 'Man with death watch beetle in wooden leg should be grateful he is not man with tin leg in thunderstorm.' But what more vengeful gratitude than the English! You spend fifty years crippling service in the Balham Gas Board Repair Shops and they give you nothing more than a crappy five-pound clock inscribed 'In Gratitude'.

Strangely though, for the early years of my life, through the

9

grammatical misuse of the word I had a complete misconception of it, due mainly to a story my father recounted of an incident in Mesopotamia during World War I . . . 'It was a dark night, and Sgt Paddy Manning heard a wounded Arab calling for water, so, at risk of his life, he crawled out of the trench to the Arab and gave him a drink of water. As soon as he turned his back the Arab shot him in the arse, now *there's* gratitude for you.' So, in those early years, I thought gratitude meant a bullet in the arse, or an act of treachery.

Not long after, father and I were watching the finals of the inter-services boxing match in Kirkee. At one stage a boxer hit his opponent below the belt and sent him cross-eyed rolling round the ring at speed. 'There's gratitude for you, Dad,' I said. I wondered why he looked puzzled.

Next there was a terrible murder in Poona. A man had gone into his sweetheart's boudoir and blown her brains out with a shotgun. 'There's gratitude for you,' I said to my Dad.

There's a delightful story of a man's kindness to an animal. At a circus, a man in the front row reached out and gave the performing elephant a banana. Two years later the circus returned. Would the elephant remember him? The man went and sat in the same seat. When the elephant came on, it saw him and came straight towards him, put its trunk round his neck and strangled him. Now, that could be called an act of ingratitude. It wasn't, it was just a different elephant. The man was Carl Foreman.

Oh yes, in Silly Willy's letter he says 'Were you grateful to Churchill?'

Me? Grateful to Churchill? What for? While he was gulping Napoleon brandy 1811, in the sun of Marrakesh, I was sipping piss-poor tea 1943 from a jam tin in a water-logged hole in Africa called the 1st Army.

CONSCIENCE: 'You swine, Milligan. He gave of his best.'

ME: 'You're right. Mr Churchill, I am very grateful to you for World War II.'

WINSTON: 'Ta.'

ME: 'Aren't you grateful to me?'

WINSTON: 'Why should I be? While I was being forced to drink Napoleon brandy in the sun of Marrakesh, you were gulping piss-poor tea in a water-logged hole in Africa.'

ADOLF HITLER: 'Silung! *I* am not grateful to *you*, Winston von Churchill!'

WINSTON: 'Well I am grateful to you! – that's how I got the job!'

ADOLF HITLER: 'I'll say, brudder! But for *me*, *you* would still be laying bricks in Chartwell. Und *I* vould be zer Queen of England.'

PRINCE PHILIP: 'I say look here, Hitler!'

ENOCH VON POWELL: 'He'd solve the Wog problem!'

You see? Gratitude is a many diversified thing. I include here visual evidence of the quality of gratitude. Here you see the Lord Snowdon photograph of Lord and Lady Beauleigh-Thucks who engaged Signor Giovanni Sapone the great Italian castrati tenor, who had had the operation just for them. He sang *Senza due Ballo* to the guests for 3 hours and then, well, see talk-bubble above. . .

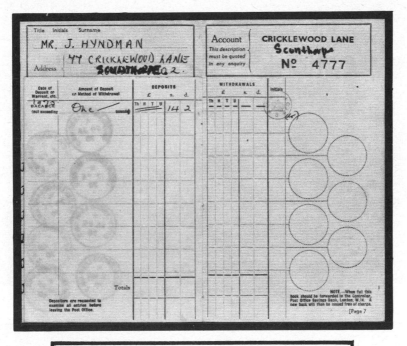

The Post Office book of Mr J. Hyndman, one of Scunthorpe's big spenders, showing his balance of 14s.2d

The Grand Spa Orchestra, Scunthorpe – Max Jaffa extreme
left out of the picture

Honesty

The Editor of *Punch*, slobbering white, comes tippy toe to me, Spike Milligna the well known typing error, and whines 'Will you write an article on Honesty?' Of course I will, anything to stop the closure of the magazine. There was the usual hand to hand struggle with pangas to agree the fee. Honesty? Of course I knew all about it, wasn't it growing in my garden under the name of *Lunaria biennis*?

It wasn't until I had finished the third volume that Silly Willy Davis pointed out the mistake. 'You silly twit, you've made a cock-up.' I accepted the apology and a cheque for eighty new pence in lieu of a court case. He went on 'You really are a sillypoo, what we want is the moral connotation. Write one thousand two hundred words.' *One thousand two hundred words?* On Honesty? Nobody was that HONEST. Twenty-seven words was enough for anyone, even Jesus, and he's a bit suspect – it's strange, *he never put anything in writing!*

HONESTY. I went to the British Museum, where they kept the word under lock and key. The word has been on loan to Mr Jack Jones, but the moment he mentioned 'HONEST day's work' he was floored by a docker. The keeper of the word HONESTY took me into its cage. 'It's getting a bit old and worn. We've tried to get a new one but it's very rare, in fact it's in the World Wildlife Fund Red Book as endangered. I think myself it's 'ad it. I sometimes take it for a walk on a lead, but nobody seemed to recognize it, some children patted it but that's all.'

'What is your opinion of the word HONEST?'

'It can't live in twentieth-century environment sir, so she's dyin', we try matin' it wiv the word PAYS, and get a sort of cross-breed called HONESTY-PAYS. We flew it in!'

'In? Where from?'

'Russia, they has this word PAYS on its own in a cage, it was a male, because the Male always PAYS.'

'Did it work?'

'No.'

In the Reading Room I looked it up. There it was. HONEST: Upright, fair, trustworthy in dealings, frank. Open. Honest to goodness, to turn an honest penny, to seize opportunity to make a profit, to make an honest woman of a seduced woman . . . so, an honest man had a military bearing (upright). Blond hair (fair). Plays cards (trustworthy dealings). Christian name Frank (frank). Doorman (open). Welsh (honest to goodness). Robs weak old ladies (seizes opportunity to make a profit). Makes single women pregnant and then marries them (To make an honest woman of a seduced woman).

Next on the list of Silly Willy's questions was:

QUESTION 1: 'Have there been times in your life when you were totally honest, and regretted it?'

ANSWER: 'Yes. I once said to a 6 ft 3 in Canadian soldier "I'll punch your bloody head in." '

QUESTION 2: 'Are there times when you wished you *had* been totally honest?'

ANSWER: 'Yes. My first marriage. I said "I do." '

QUESTION 3: 'What sort of things on the national scene etc. do you think we should be totally honest about?'

ANSWER: 'All those faceless bastards called "Spokesman Said" should be forced to give their names i.e. "A Spokesman Said called The Hon. Startling-Grope OBE said etc. etc." '

And who cares about honesty in this day and age? Diogenes walked the streets of Athens in daylight holding aloft a lamp to help him find an honest man. Imagine that in Piccadilly.

POLICEMAN: 'I saw the accused, Diogenes, at midday in Piccadilly carrying a hurricane lamp, which he held up in the face of oncoming men.'

JUDGE: 'Is that true?'

DIOGENES: 'Yes. I was looking for an honest man.'
JUDGE: 'In London?'
DIOGENES: 'Yes.'
JUDGE: 'Remanded for a psychiatric report.'

And take the first American President. There he is as a lad, a fresh felled cherry tree lies at his feet, he is clutching a hot axe, not another person for miles when a man asks:

MAN: 'Son, who chopped down the cherry tree?'
GEORGE: 'I cannot tell a lie, I did.'

I mean, what *else* could he say? And because of that he's called honest? And why is it that those in dodgy professions use the word? The bookie 'Honest' Bill Hampton? A glance down shows him to be wearing running shoes. Why not extend the idea? . . .

BBC TV ANNOUNCER: 'And now a partially political broadcast by Honest Reginald Maudling . . .'

Or 'And now our annual company report by Honest Sir Val Duncan.' Why should the world only apply to homo sapiens? Why not, 'Look out here comes HONEST Tiger,' or 'Help, I am being strangled by HONEST Gorilla'? Let's break the word down into units. Take H, Hitler, Hum-drum, Hack, Horrible, or HO, Ho Ho Ho, mocking laughter, three letters HON, the HON Edward Heath, see? It leads to a twit.

No, we need a new word. I suggest Eileen. 'That man's one of the most EILEEN men in the world', or 'He's never done an EILEEN day's work in his life.'

Well, that should keep Silly Willy quiet for a while. And I say to you all, try and live an EILEEN life. That's the best I can do, Willy. EILEEN it is.

Some Like It Hot

There are many ways of keeping warm. It all depends on how much money you have. Let's start at the bottom, that is the bottom of the social scale. There are those gentlemen of the road who at midnight can be seen sleeping peacefully on the embankment in cold weather. The secret is the English Newspaper, which is wrapped around the inside of the outergarments, the *Financial Times* being a favourite; as one tramp said, 'Like bein' wrapped in dreams.'

I myself was working-class and keeping warm was different in each room. The outside WC in winter was a formidable affair, so when I saw my father putting on long underwear, a heavy sweater, overcoat, muffler and gloves I knew what his next function was. My brother had his own method: he would do vigorous exercises until he was boiling hot, then rush to the WC, abort at speed and get back before he grew cold. The only room with heat was the kitchen where a great iron stove glowed red, fed with all the rubbish in the house; on its hot plate kettles steamed and whistled, pots boiled, conkers hardened, chestnuts popped and socks and underwear steamed in the scarlet heat, and grandma's shins scorched in the inferno. No, there was no heating problem for the poor in the kitchen, but the rest of the home was clutched in Stygian ice.

The habit of staying up late only came into being when people stopped sleeping in the kitchen or, to be exact, in pre-industrial times the kitchen, bedroom and living-room were all one room. But came the age of the separate bedroom and late nights started. My own family would start to disrobe in the kitchen, start putting on flannelette nightshirts, pyjamas, bed socks etc., and finally, each one clutching a hot water bottle, we would get on our marks and at a signal run screaming to our freezing beds, from where we would all groan and scream 'O Christ I'm freezin', cor stone a crow, Brrrrrrrrr, etc., etc.,' until the bed became warm. Winter mornings were agony; the thought of getting out of bed was as pleasant as hara-kiri. So I would pull my suit into bed and, when it was warm, undress and dress under the bedclothes; mind you my suit looked like a concertina, but I was warm.

Now the article is about keeping warm, so let's bring it into the present. I give up. I don't know *how* to keep warm. Keeping warm with central heating is very difficult, because most of the time is spent roasting. As a result one spends the evening adjusting the thermostat, opening and closing windows, taking off jackets or pullovers, so there is as much difficulty keeping warm with central heating as if you were in a freezing room. If it were up to me, I would abolish all central heating; it destroys furniture, floors, walls, and your respiratory system. No, a big cosy armchair, a pair of thick woollen socks, carpet slippers and a roaring coal fire (or logs) are the answer. In the street, people only get cold if they walk like cripples (as most of the English do). I walk very fast; as a result I arrive at work warm as toast and exhausted for the day.

A popular tomb in Scunthorpe
(*by permission of Mrs Thrills*)

17

* Pull Down St. Paul's!

Headline in the *Peking Bulletin:* 'English Minister of Transport buys 600 Disused Old Chinese Trams.' As the Minister of Transport so wisely said at the time: 'You never know, we might need them.' It is in this fine tradition that we find that splendid autocrat Sir Keith Joseph, who will for ever be remembered as the Englishman who did as much for British architecture in London as Attila did for Roman cities. Which brings us to Juxon House.

To date, all we have heard are the asinine criticisms of those who are concerned only with the west face of St Paul's. St Paul's indeed! Are they blind to the beauties of Juxon House? Thank heaven there are those who are not, in particular the architect, the builders, the shareholders and the owners, who are all very aware of the new jewel that is raising its clean head in Ludgate Hill.

I am glad to report that the Minister of Housing is being approached with a complaint that St Paul's is in fact obscuring the new office block's south-west front! He will be requested to pull down part of St Paul's to afford the public a better view of the building.

For reasons beyond logic, Sir Keith, after considering the idea, said: 'While sympathizing with them, the idea was financially not practicable, and it appeared that the public might be strongly averse to such a move.'

In a moment of *laisser-faire*, I phoned the Ministry and asked to speak to the Press representative. After several to eight minutes I was passed to a man called 'Spokesman Said'. I asked him was the Minister likely to stop the building of Juxon House?

SPOKESMAN SAID: 'No.'

ME: 'Why was the plan passed in the first place?'

SPOKESMAN SAID: 'It's very simple.'

*see also *Sink the Bismarck* and *Raise the Titanic!*

18

ME: 'I know that.'

SPOKESMAN SAID: 'It's very simple. The building was placed in its present position for historical and commemorative reasons. Juxon House has been built on its present site because it is the identical spot on which Bishop Juxon stood to admire St Paul's west face. That is also why the building is called Juxon House.'

ME: 'Splendid. But did not the Minister know that public opinion was in favour of building being suspended prior to an inquiry?'

SPOKESMAN SAID: 'Yes, but what the public did not know was that but for Sir Keith's timely intervention, St Paul's might be no more.'

ME: 'Exploon that?' (Yes, exploon!)

SPOKESMAN SAID: 'The original company had plans to pull the cathedral down and build a block of self-contained St Paul's Cathedrals.'

ME: 'Gloria in Excelsis.'

SPOKESMAN SAID: 'I'm sorry, that's for the Foreign Office to answer. What did you say your name was?'

ME: 'Spokesman Listening.'

Thus ended the conversation. Mulling it over in my mind, stomach, and knees, I realized if this present state of objections continued we could get headlines like this: 'LTE to sue Balham Gasworks. South Face of Trolleybus Depot in Pratts Road in danger of being Obscured by new Gasometer. LTE appeal to public: "Save your Balham Bus Depot from visual Vandalism." '

The whole problem of obscuring will certainly divide the country in two, i.e., People versus the Government. To back up the falling prestige of the Ministry of Housing, the Government might encourage Art to abandon chiaroscuro and settle for oscuro alone.

But let us move forward in time and think of St Paul's 500 years hence, that is, in another 10 Sir Keith Josephs from now. Allowing that further uncontrolled building will continue in and around St Paul's, the official tourist brochure will read like this:

Those wishing to obtain the best view of the west face should apply to the chairman of the Imprudential (whose offices stretch right across the forecourt of St Paul's – see plan above) enclosing a 25p postal order. You will be sent

19

a ticket overstamped 'Visitor. West Front.' This entitles the holder to enter the Imprudential office block, take the lift to the seventeenth floor, where, through the window in a janitor's cupboard, a reasonable view can be had. A complete view can be obtained by photographing those areas visible from office numbers 5, 6, 7, 10, 13, 18 and 20, and piecing them together.

Owing to the heavy shadow cast by the Impru offices, it is advisable to carry a hand torch. Those who cannot afford the postal order can do it all free by following these instructions: walk to the back of the 80-storey office block directly in front of St Paul's; there you will find a narrow alley two feet wide; on your left will be the back of the Impru, and on your right the steps of the west face of St Paul's; lie on your left side facing the step. Turn the head three inches to the right, at the same time craning the neck slightly to the left; cast your eyes to the extreme right and then look slightly up; now hold a small hand-mirror approximately six inches from the face, moving the mirror slowly from 45 to 60 degrees, where it will reflect a fine view of the west face. For those with money to spare the LTE has laid on a special helicopter which takes up to eight passengers. Each passenger in turn is lowered between the Impru and the cathedral in a wicker basket and flown backwards and forwards along the narrow alley, allowing a panoramic view.

I think what the present Sir Keith Joseph has in mind is to enclose St Paul's on all sides thus creating a modern Petra and giving it an air of Eastern mystery.

Sir Keith sees a future in which special guides, chosen for their likeness to Sir Christopher Wren, and dressed in the costume of the period, will carry flaming brands and conduct tourists on horse-back down the narrow, ink-black alleys, showing the mysterious and permanently hidden north, south, east and west fronts.

So think twice, irate citizens, ere you condemn Juxon House. As the Queen would say: 'God bless Sir Keith and all who fail in him.'

Exit Milligan pursued by a bear.

Not Again? !

Aristocrats have heirs; the poor have children; the rest keep dogs. It's high time we paid attention to the English Dog Cult, which now vies with Christianity in the top ten religions.

There was a time when the forebears of the contemporary dog ran free in packs of up to a hundred; a short, stocky yellow-haired fellow, hunting and living as he pleased, enjoying the primitive freedom of a collar-free throat. It's hard to believe that the lump of hairy fat slobbed out in front of a Belgravia fire is a direct descendant of that once noble creature. 'Where walk humans, there walks corruption.'

Back in the mists of time, there fell from a tree a half-upright hairy creature called Man. Later on some were called Women. This eased the Paleolithic sexual frustration which, up till then, had been called the Ice Age (in my district it looks like coming back; we had a beauty contest last week and nobody won it). Feasting on a mish-mash of mammoth, chips and Flag sauce, early man moved on, leaving in his wake a trail of bones, scrag ends and unconscious bachelors who had overdone the spring fertility rites.

Lying there naked, daubed with woad
and feathers, they looked, as we say,
  done up like a dog's dinner,
    which in fact they became.

AWWWWWW !wwww

From then on, the more wayward of the dog pack scavenged in the van of the itinerant early tribes. In the cold winter of his discontent, man, by striking trees with lightning, invented (a) fire and (b) nothing else. Wayward dog drew near the crackling flames and stretched his body in the effulgent warmth; unwittingly he was taking the first steps to the lush life of social elevation and canine oblivion.

Dog grew sleeker, fatter; his fleas became an affluent society. Dog even learned to wag his tail; it seemed to please his master, but always puzzled the dog. His bitch bore a litter of twelve yellow, flop-eared, wobbly pups.

Now it came to pass that among the busy tribe there was one wayward, less industrious female. This lass came upon what up till then had been a perfectly happy litter; she bent down (a dangerous pastime in that period) and picked up one of the pups.

'Awwwwwwwwwwww,' she said.

From that moment on, the creature called Dog was doomed. Through the ensuing centuries he has been interbred, cross-bred, inbred, overbred, stretched, reduced, lengthened, shortened, his face pushed in to make his eyes pop, hair grown over his eyes to blind him, tail lopped off, ears clipped; and latterly he has been fired to the moon. Today, the creature has lost all knowledge of what he really is; the saving grace is the mongrel (thank God for him!), who is, of course, shunned by the canine hierarchy.

The female adulation of the dog puzzled many sociologists; then Freud made it clear: 'What you can't impose on a man, you can always impose on a dog' (and vice versa). Nowadays, the neurotic descendants of the once wild dog can be seen in Royal Parks being escorted by white, pinched-faced Maudie Littlehamptons; that, or ensconced in the back of a Rolls-Bentley, with the window down to allow the beast freedom to bark at us less fortunate pavement travellers; and/or under tables in expensive restaurants, where they crunch the ankles of passing waiters and collect scraps of scampi from the plate of the owner.

Since 1945, a bundle of yapping nerves with hair on called a poodle has become the status symbol of the top OK people. Shorn in the most grotesque manner, this breed sports manicured claws, shampooed coats with a champagne rinse, little leather bootees, and the latest from America – an electrically heated doggy jacket, with the wire built into the lead and the batteries, complete with thermostat, in the owner's handbag or pocket.

Industries devoted exclusively to the canine gourmet are quoted on the Stock Exchange; on TV: 'Don't let *your* dog eat the same scraps as you do. Give him Woof-A, the dog food with the built-in linger-longer hormone Vitamin,' and in Queensway (I could hardly believe it), 'Make your dog happy with "The Meat-flavoured Nylon Play Bone." ' (This is the real stuff of humanity; how about 'Milk-flavoured wood chips for the starving children in the Congo'?)

Miniatures. This is a dog that at one time stood 14 feet high and through the centuries has been reduced to a convenient size to insert in pockets, handbags, shopping baskets or dustbins. These are very rarely allowed to walk; of course, some of the better breeds don't know how to.

You can see the whole lunatic menagerie any morning after 10.30 in the vicinity of the Round Pond, Kensington. While little children are being strapped down in prams, incarcerated in reins, sat on, hit, shouted at and generally terrorized, dogs are allowed to bite, chew, leap at old ladies, terrify, eat wild ducks, copulate and urinate at will. All these cavortings are watched by the adoring owners who pass little maternal messages, 'I *do* like him to play with dogs of his own age' and/or 'Have you put his name down for Crufts yet?', and, of course, 'He knows *every word you say*.'

I shall never forget the spectacle that fine spring morning when, opposite the Horse Guards Barracks, an off-white Mercedes suffering from diplomatic immunity pulled to a Teutonic halt. A liveried chauffeur opened the back door and from a cushion picked up what I can describe only as a piece of knotted string with legs, carrying it like the Crown Jewels. He crossed Rotten Row and deposited the creature on the grass, where it sat for an hour blinking in the unaccustomed sunlight. From the rear window of the car a doting, ageing Brunnhilde watched its every move through a pair of opera glasses.
One's spirits soar at this gesture of man's selfless devotion to his dog.

What happens to these vivacious thoroughbreds when they age? On grim winter evenings, when streets are deserted, through the back alleys of Belgravia, Knightsbridge and Kensington, you will see two shadowy figures moving painfully down a dark street. They move arthritically in the gloom. One is a fat, waddling, wheezy dog, one-time champion, now a grey-muzzled, dim-eyed, has-been. And walking ten respectful paces behind him, another grey-muzzled, dim-eyed has-been of a man. Both are the discards of one woman. Sadly they tread the pavements; in their wake usually follows a series of small posters. 'A fine of £5 will be imposed on the owner of any dog that is allowed to foul the pavements.'

Back home, madam is bending down to pick up a new black poodle puppy. 'Awwwwwwwwwwwww,' she says. And that's where I came in.

Going, Going...

It is now 46 years since World War II, since when there has been one long permanent rehearsal for World War III. (Book now – trenches in all parts.) Korea, Tibet, Suez, Indo-China, Kenya, Hungary, Algeria, Congo, Somaliland, Cyprus, Vietnam, Angola, Kashmir, all called 'local wars'. (Yes folks! Keep your wars local and save world peace.)

In this welter of human folly another small world of pain and blood passes almost unnoticed – the gradual destruction of the oldest kingdom on earth, that of the wild animal. For the first time since the mysterious disappearance of the mighty and seemingly indestructible dinosaurs, such as *Tyrannosaurus Rex*, wild life is in danger of complete extinction. Having survived more than 30 million years of evolution birds are vanishing from the sky, fish from the sea and animals from the earth. Since 1900, 100 species of wild creatures have become extinct.

Four-fifths of the world's population have little or no real understanding of wild animals. The remaining fifth includes a mixture of people who dote on cats and dogs, sending them to poodle parlours, etc., etc. In Australia, kangaroos are being slaughtered wholesale (or is it re-tail?), especially for doggy food, without a whisper of complaint from the doggy lovers.

What has happened? The Industrial Revolution and the population explosion reduced rural and natural confines. At the same time millions cut themselves off from both, concentrating in smoky concrete jungles called 'cities'. Within them families were born, lived and died, seeing no creature wilder than the horse (with motor cars, even that link has disappeared). And so it came to pass, man no longer hunted animal for food, and thus lost respect for his ancient prey. Gone was the once timeless mystique of the hunter and hunted. Nevertheless, the ancient desire for Western man to hunt was still deep-rooted, but, since there was no cogent reason to do so, to salve his conscience and facilitate a primitive desire, he invented hunting for 'sport' – that or the fox-hunters old hollow argument of 'Keeping them down'.

On now to the Bulwark of Democracy – America, Ta-raa! The American bison, the greatest land bank of meat on the hoof man has ever known, was shot to the verge of extinction for profit or sport. Special trains were chartered, the carriages full of 'sportsmen'. Cowboys drove the herds towards the guns, and corpses lay rotting in the sun. That was 70 years ago. What have we learnt? After the war, Yemeni sheikhs started to drive motorcades of Cadillacs into herds of Arabian oryx and to slaughter them with machine-guns. By 1962 the oryx was all but extinct.

Did no one care? Did no one remember the Creator's words to Noah? The lesson of the Ark? There was a very slender ray of hope. A few sad but courageous men had built a small, modern ark called the World Wildlife Fund. With a limited amount of money and armed mostly with hope, they worked not only against the clock but against the apathy of a society that is laughingly called 'Christian'.

With a borrowed army helicopter, a Land-Rover, and with a few helpers, Major Peter Raven did the impossible. In the appalling heat of the Yemen, three oryx, two bucks and one doe, were captured alive. I won't recount the myriad red-tape difficulties that beset animal preservationists, but the oryx were taken to Phoenix, Arizona, which has a similar climate to that of the Yemen. In October 1963 a male oryx calf was born. His picture appeared in several daily newspapers, and there was no shortage of those who stood on the sidelines and said: 'Awwww . . . isn't he sweet', and did little else.

All this rescue work was being done in the face of great financial difficulties. Was there money from the famous 'Foundations' for this and that? Not a penny. About the time the oryx rescue was going on, the public of dear old England had been coaxed into giving £350,000 towards buying a Leonardo cartoon which was in 'danger' of being bought abroad (up till then it had been kept in a cellar). The Government added another £450,000 to clinch the deal.

£800,000! With that sort of money the future of *living* master-pieces, that not even Leonardo could create, might be secured: the orang-utan, the panda, the Javan rhino, the cheetah, the whooping crane, the Tasmanian tiger. The fight for wild life is no crank struggle: it is as much a battle to save man's morality as it is to save the world of animals he is constantly destroying.

Don't wait. Do something *now* – otherwise future visits to the zoo will be to 'See the Plastic Elephants.' 'This way to the clock-work chimps' tea-party.' 'Come and pop the inflatable rubber hippos.' 'See the radar-controlled wooden pelicans.' I am donating the fee for this article to the World Wildlife Fund. What are *you* going to do? Stroke Pussy?

A young merry lad
in Scunthorpe

Read All About It!

Let me take you back to India circa 1924. (Try dialling it, you get put through right away.) It was a period when a khaki copy of *The Times* flew alongside the Union Jack at Government House. I was 7 at the time. Every morning at Reveille a Coggage Wallah* delivered the *Poona Times*, which I dutifully took to my bed-ridden, dying grandfather. In those early years I thought a news-paper was something you gave to dying grandfathers. Having just read the entire range of morning papers, I am still of the opinion it is something you give to dying grandfathers. Hindu editors never quite got the hang of our language, for example the headline: GANDHI SENT TO YERODAH GAOL. SERVES HIM JOLLY WELL RIGHT.' And again the same week: 'GANDHI THREATENS HUNGER STRIKE: KING GEORGE VERY ANGRY GOD BLESS HIM.'

I still retain cuttings of my father's theatrical exploits in India. The *Bangalore Cantonment Gazette*: 'Bombadier and Mrs Leo Milligan, the married couple, were the hitting of the night' and, further on, 'Mr Bertram Kettleband did very fine readings from Charles Dickens' *Great Expectorations*.' Once a month we would receive the Overseas *Daily Mirror*, in its gamboge cover.

My early knowledge of England then was through the headlines. I thought an ordinary day in England was 'Heavy Snow in Cots-wolds. Villagers cut off. Sheep Starving. Jimmy Wilde Champion of the World. King George Gravely Ill. Desperate Unemployment in Wales. Gracie Fields Mobbed. Fol de Rols break all records in Eastbourne. Beheaded Nude Body of Woman found on Brighton Beach.' The only normal thing in the paper was Pip Squeak and

* *Paper boy.*

28

A black gentleman with his dinner

Mrs Thrills's boarding house cat, Mr Crippen

Wilfred. It was a shock when I arrived in England to find that people in the street were not penguins, dogs or rabbits. This made me sad, as I was a member of the Gugnunk Club. I was 13 at the time. Sitting on the train from Tilbury to London I saw the headline: 'DOCKS. RAMSAY MACDONALD STEPS IN.'

My own father went to work for the Associated Press of America off Fleet Street, and was soon on the bottle and murmuring: 'There's a nasty rumour going around Fleet Street and his name is Lord Northcliffe!' During his delirium he made up headlines. 'Titanic arrives safe at Southampton. "I overslept," says Captain,' or 'Archduke Ferdinand still alive! World War I a Mistake! Sorry says Kaiser.' He told me that every night news editors knelt naked in front of a statue of Beaverbrook, crossed themselves with printers' ink and said, 'Please God may something terrible happen in the world tonight preferably to (a) the King, (b) the Pope, or (c) Jack Buchanan, and please in time for the next edition, eh?'

I was 14 at the time. It's on record that the old editor of the now dead *News Chronicle* was without a morning headline and lay face down on the floor chewing the carpet. The phone rang, 'Hello Dad? Brace yourself. Mother's just been killed by a coloured Chinese Jew who plays the trombone in Harry Roy's band.' 'Thank God,' said the editor, 'I'll have a photographer round in a flash.'

In those days newspapers did straightforward reporting, i.e. a football match was reported on the merits of the game. Not so today. The reporter concentrates on the player–manager–dressing-room–boardroom conflicts. You don't report goals, you report punch-ups. A Rangers-Celtic match is now reported: Rangers: 3 dead, 20 injured. Celtic: 7 injured, 1 dead.' The unruly player gets the news. Let's take George Best. He arrives 10 minutes late for practice; 'GEORGE BEST MISSING! "I don't know where he is," says sexy 23-year-old Pop Star Sandra O'Toole, son of Peter O'Toole, who is also missing from his grave in Highgate Old Cemetery where is making *Carry on Up Your Dracula*.' When Best arrives ten minutes later: 'BEST GIVES HIMSELF UP!' says the midday edition. 'Under questioning from hard-hitting team manager Jim 'Socks' Scrackle, "Best broke down and confessed that he was 10 minutes late." ' 'BEST CONFESSES! "Ten Minutes That Nearly Ruined My Life." Read all about it in the *News of the World*. The newspaper with its heart in your knickers.'

There is a surfeit of news in England, unlike my parents' bush town in Australia, Woy Woy. Nothing happens in Woy Woy. Some headlines are desperate: 'TODAY IS THE 3RD OF APRIL. OFFICIAL.' Cub reporters try and turn minutiae into leaders. 'Woy Woy. April 10. This morning during Woy Woy's rush hour, a Mrs Glenda Scrock, 64-year-old housewife, was standing at the corner of Kitchener Avenue and Bindi Bindi Crescent when she saw a broken pencil lying on the pavement. She picked it up. It was a 2B. She threw the pencil in the gutter. The police have ruled out foul play.' The fact that Harry Secombe arrived at Woy Woy station with a banner saying 'I AM HARRY SECOMBE' and went unrecognized is by the way.

Let's look at the character of each British newspaper each covering the same story. Let us imagine that Princess Anne, like Sir Stafford Cripps' daughter, married a coloured man, say an African goat herder.

Morning Star
MARRIAGE OF CONVENIENCE.
CUNNING MOVE BY
HEATH
GOVERNMENT TO PLACATE
BLACK RHODESIANS

Daily Telegraph
COLOURFUL ROYAL
WEDDING

It was announced from the Palace today that Her Royal Highness is to marry Mr N'galu N'Goolie, a foreign gentleman with farming connections in Africa, his dark skin no doubt the result of long hours in the tropical sun supervising his herds.

Financial Times
SOUND FINANCIAL MOVE
BY ROYAL FAMILY

The forthcoming marriage of Princess Anne to a PAYE native Rhodesian commoner will entitle her to £100,000 from the privy purse as a married woman. Her husband's goat herd will be put in her name. The Goats will go public next year as Royal Goat Herd (Holdings) Limited.

31

Sun
IT'S A WHITE AND BLACK
WEDDING FOR ANNE

Private Eye
PRINCESS ANNE
REQUESTS
PERMISSION TO MARRY
WOG SHEPHERD.
OPTICIAN ROYAL
CALLED TO PALACE

No more coloured TV for her says angry Philip. When the royal parents were informed of their daughter's wishes, the husband presumptive, a Mr N'galu N'Goolie, was rushed to Buckingham Palace where surgeons worked on him all night with powerful bleaches. This morning his condition was described as 'fair'.

Daily Mail
IT'S HATS OFF TO
ANOTHER ROYAL FIRST

Our sporting Princess is to marry a dashing dusky African goat herder. During her *Blue Peter* trip, our sporting Princess fell in love with dashing 5ft 8in Masai, N'Goolie Esq. A spokesman at the Palace said: 'They met by accident. She ran over him in a Land-Rover.'

The Times

Reports are coming in from our foreign correspondent that Her Royal Highness Princess Anne is unwell. Reuter.

There is no more to say about the Press. If there is, you say it.

A Proverb A Week... ...

Absence makes the heart grow fonder: This is a mistake; it was misquoted by a drunken Frenchman. What he should have said was, 'Absinthe makes the heart grow fonder', or 'Absent kidneys make the heart grow larger.' (This can be verified on any railway timetable.)

Actions speak louder than words: Yes, this is perfectly true – take the action of the Royal Artillery at Tel el Kibir. During this action nobody heard a word being spoken because of the noise of the action.

All's fair in love and war: A lie – both Cleopatra and Adolf Hitler were dark. (This can be verified on any Southern Railway poster.)

All roads lead to Rome: Nonsense, how do you think I get home to Finchley?

All work and no play makes Jack a dull boy: True, as any Jack Jones record will prove.

The apples on the other side of the wall are sweetest: Wrong: apples do not grown on the sides of walls.

Better be an old man's darling than a young man's slave: Why have either of them? Try someone in the middle who won't give you a hard time. This means somebody partially bald with about £17 in the Post Office and one leg in the grave.

Better late than never: Rubbish, if you never show up, you'll never be late.

33

A bird in the hand is worth two in the bush: This is another misquote, which should read 'A bird in the Strand is better value than two birds in Shepherds Bush.'

Blood is thicker than water: Only if you add cornflour and Bovril.

Cherchez la femme: Which, as far as I know, means 'Search that woman before it's too late. Lighting-up time 7.25 p.m.'

Cleanliness is next to godliness: Oh yeah? Ask any Irish priest where the launderette is. I've never seen a launderette next to a church.

Don't change horses in mid-stream: Supposing the one you are on can't swim?

Don't have too many irons in the fire: Some people can't help it. Take Mr J. Fernanigan Flick, blacksmith, whose forge burnt down.

Don't put all your eggs in one basket: Sound advice – never wear jockey pants.

It is useless to flog a dead horse: Rubbish, take all the money you can get for it.

Don't wash your dirty linen in public: Ask an Irish priest where the launderette is.

Dog does not eat dog: Nonsense, mine has just eaten his PAL.

The early bird catches the worm: Yes, all the birds in my garden have got worms, they shouldn't get up so early.

Faint heart ne'er won fair lady: Nor a faint gall-bladder, in fact. No faint organs have ever won a fair lady.

He who hesitates is lost: Very difficult to believe. I have hesitated in the following towns – Acton, Edgware, Kilburn East – and never been lost.

Don't count your chickens before they're hatched: As I have told you before, wear jockey pants but allow for movement.

A fool and his money are soon parted: 'Ladbroke's Annual Report.'

Forbidden fruit is sweetest: I've never been forbidden to eat fruit so I wouldn't know.

The gods send nuts to those who have no teeth: They also send teeth to those who have no nuts.

Don't take your harp to a party: Nonsense, drink all you can.

Discretion is the better part of valour: The other parts are called: 'Run for it', 'Help', 'I surrender', and 'Christ! Here they come again.'

Rome was not built in a day: No, it actually took 3 weeks – the bricks were late arriving.

If the mountain will not come to Mahomet, then Mahomet must go to the mountain: A 137a bus will take him right there.

'Tis better to give than to take: Like a thud on a jaw.

Jack of all trades is master of none: David Frost.

Laugh and the world laughs with you: Ha ha ha ha ha ha ... where's everybody gone?

The leopard can't change his spots: Not at the present rate of exchange.

Money is the root of all evil: That is why Catholic priests use Barclaycards.

Muck and money go together: Go where?

Two heads are better than one: True, but who's going to marry you?

You cannot burn the candle at both ends: Yes, you can, provided you hold it in the middle.

You cannot have your cake and eat it: Rubbish, how can you eat it if you haven't got it?

Let Me Out!

It doesn't take much to start a crowd – an Irish Catholic couple can start a crowd in as little as nine months, and Pakistanis do even better. Invited to dinner with my friend Abdul Latif, I went to hang my coat in the closet and a crowd fell out. How big is a crowd? Ten? Twenty? There's no answer; ask a country yokel, he'll say, 'Arrr, a crowd is when there's two people, and neither of them is me.' To me Harry Secombe is a crowd (at sea he's a danger to shipping). Secombe as a crowd is tolerable, but imagine a crowd of Lord Longfords, or Robin Days. When does one person become a group and how many in a group before it becomes a crowd? Policemen are asked to 'Move a crowd on', but supposing they're one short of a crowd? Do they go to a bystander and say, 'Pardon me sir, can you step into this group that I may move it on as a crowd'? And only homo sapiens can be designated as A Crowd; one never hears of a crowd of Fish, e.g. if your footman approaches you and says, 'Me Lord, there's a crowd of fish on the lawn', he's a liar. Now, this article was generated by William Davis demanding answers to the crowd problem. Let's give them.

WILLIAM: 'How do you cope with a crowd?'
SPIKE: 'See handbook on Hiroshima and Nagasaki.'
WILLIAM: 'How do you stand out in a crowd?'
SPIKE: 'Stand on soap box, remove all clothing'

Crowds have only become manifest since the Industrial Revolution. In Quantums it goes, COPULATION = POPULATION = CROWDS, so stop it folks, try sucking a sweet instead, the Crowd

Hirohito opening a new Datsun factory in Scunthorpe; note Soya sauce stock on shelf placed there by Mrs Thrills

fever is on us, we are getting used to it, it's terrible, what about after life? I mean there's more people there than alive here; I don't want to go to heaven if you have to stand all the time! War is another good time for Crowds. In 1914 Crowds gathered at Buck House and cheered, Crowds queued for Food and cheered, Crowds joined the Army and Cheered, Crowds Cheered the Crowds of Troops off to France, where Crowds of Germans shot them, Crowds on both sides were killed, Crowds of cowards ran like the clappers. Some found it difficult to be a Crowd; both the Kaiser and George V said, 'I'm sorry, my people, that I too am not a Crowd', and the Crowds cheered, but *individuals* who refused to fight were shot, so they too ended up in Crowded War Cemeteries. There's *no* escape, you've *got* to be in a Crowd.

It's unavoidable, you wake up as an individual at 7.30. Forty minutes later you are part of an asphyxiated Crowd on a tube train, at Marble Arch sheer bulk forces you off the train, even though your destination is Charing Cross. I was born Crowd free in the open plains of India; the only Crowds I saw were British Regiments on their way to saw through Gandhi's legs. In 1933 the Labour Government decided to make a 10 per cent cut in the Indian Army, so my father, in the middle of a military career and lunch, had 10 per cent of his shin sawn off and stumped unfit for duty. My first moments of Crowding were about to start, we were packed in a crate labelled SS RAJPURNA, SOLDIER'S FAMILY, THIS WAY UP. The accommodation on the ship is best described by my drawing of the time.

Arriving in England in Crowds we queued to get in. Since then I've watched the British people accept and finally cry out to be in Crowds. Example:

A Harley Street doctor's consulting room.
    DOCTOR: *'Next, please.'*
    Enter a male, shattered wreck in the corner of some foreign suit that is forever England.
    MAN: *'Doctor, I've got to get into a Crowd soon, I'm suffering withdrawal symptoms.'*
    DOCTOR: *'I'll start by just giving you this bill for five guineas, and here is a prescription for you to stand in Crowds three times a day*

38

after meals. Meantime I want you to take these tablets that will leave you with the feeling you are being crushed.'

MAN: *'God bless you, doctor.'*

DOCTOR: *'Another five guineas please.'*

> *Some enchanted evening*
> *You may see a stranger*
> *You may see a stranger*
> *Across a Crowded room.*

Someone should tell Hammerstein you can't see across a crowded room, not even a stranger. The craving for Crowds exists after office hours. Every evening thousands of people take one small room, two bottles of filthy sherry, pack room to suffocation and *voilà!* a cocktail party. On such an occasion I left a lady to get her a drink; the next time I heard of her was eight years later, from Brazil, and it's going to get worse, chum. We are due, like the stars, for *Super*-Crowd.

The year 1987! Sunday, and by mid-day commuters are starting to suffer the agonies of Crowd withdrawal. To alleviate this, LPTB lay on special Sunday therapeutic trains; sufferers mass on the platforms, and hydraulically operated machines will squash the victims into every inch of carriage. At the next stop, when it would appear there is no more room, the next Crowd will be forced in with powerful air jets; those unable to find room will be smeared with grease and slid between the legs of those left standing. And off again. By now the sufferers are feeling better. At the next station the driver slams the brakes on, shooting everyone up to one end. At that moment hundreds more are fired in from pressurized air cannons into the new-found space. Further cramming is possible as the roofs are made of rubber and standing on each other's shoulders is possible. 'You can't pack any more on the train,' you say, but remember, Super-Crowd! At the very next station, the train is sprayed with a powerful adhesive glue and fresh passengers are stuck to the outside.

So *now*, are you all aware of the danger of Crowds? Crowds are good for some people. Others reach a level where they don't have to be in them, like Tom Jones, but let him turn up at the Gold

Nugget in Las Vegas and the place is empty, and Tom Jones is a changed man. Again, a colonel shouting, 'About turn' to an empty parade ground shows how desperate is his need for a Crowd of Irish Guards. The day will come when BBC TV will be forced to give forecasts:

BBC FORECASTER: Good evening, here is a Crowd warning. There are Crowds strength seven here, here, here and here, and a very large Crowd just north of Ealing. Several large Crowds are expected south of the Thames, but should disperse towards evening. There is a Crowd warning for Bournemouth where Crowds of Hindu families are congregating for their annual fertility rite, but they should go by late evening leaving just a few infuriated colonels.

The writing is on the wall, folks, Crowds are in, and *you* are one of them.

A dog begging in Scunthorpe

Christmas Comes Once Too Much a Year

Christmas – the word strikes fear in every Christian adult. A time of good cheer – yes – but what does it add up to? So far mine adds up to £182. Is there any more spine-chilling remark than the wife saying, 'About the presents this year, dear'? That simple remark, that was once delivered about three weeks prior to the happy day, is now mentioned in November; one starts buying fireworks with holly on.

When *I* was a child my presents were two boxes of lead soldiers – but now my children's list starts thus:

Jane (8) – Honda motor boke.
Sile (16) – Quadrophonic hi-fi sound kit.

I tell you, there should be a Minister of Christmases! Laws:

(1) It is forbidden to spend more than £2 per present per person.
(2) One is *not* obliged to kiss any woman under the mistletoe.
(3) Christmas cards must be sent only to close relatives.

When I think of the insane, frenzied shopping on the 23rd and 24th – by the 25th, 60 per cent of the nation's shoppers are in a state of collapse and about to be aroused at 0500 hours on the dawn of the 25th. I myself have been woken at 3 o'clock with the blowing of bugles, beating of drums, squeaking and barking toys. By the night of the 26th I am adding codicils to my will: 'I leave *nothing* to *any* of my family, they've already got enough.'

My list of Christmas cards runs into 600 people – half of them unknown. For instance, about 1959 I received a Christmas card with a snap of a baby, signed 'Merry Christmas from Fred and

Family', no address. Next year, the same baby one year older. 'Merry Christmas Fred and family'. Last year the card had six of his kids on – 'Merry Christmas Fred and family'. Every Christmas I want to send him a card but I don't know *who* or where he is, and there are a hundred like him. They sign themselves 'Jim and Mary' as though they were the only Jim and Mary in the world!

I believe it to be the work of one man, who is a sadist, and gloats at my discomfort; his name might even be Tom, Jim or Mary.

And when Christmas morning arrives, that voice says, 'Hurry up dear, the children are waiting to open the presents on the Christmas tree.' Dying of fatigue, you arrive in the front room full of smiling faces, you in that 28-year-old dressing-gown, with 7-year-old C and A slippers held on with string, unshaven. You force a smile that cripples your face. 'And here's one for Daddy.' You unwrap a plastic battery-operated fish with flashing eyes – Love from Jane. 'Do you like it, Daddy – I saved up and bought it myself,' she says. What can you say but, 'It's lovely, darling.' There's 50 slim cigars; you gave up smoking 8 years ago. Two bottles of after-shave; you haven't shaved for 5 years. Your vagrant son and daughter arrive; more cigars, shaving lotion.

'Oh, lovely,' you say. A late Christmas card arrives: 'A Merry Christmas from the Manager and Staff of Coutts' – the writing is in red. As a vegetarian, something is bothering me – the Turkey dinner.

TURKEY: 'Aren't you ashamed?'

ME: 'Yes. I'm sorry I'm going to eat you.'

TURKEY: '*You're* sorry.'

ME: 'Be reasonable. All my children will be here. If I don't join the festivities they think of me as a Scrooge Father.'

TURKEY: '*I'm* a father. I left behind a wife and six kids!'

ME: 'Look, I promise this will be the *last* Christmas I'll eat you.'

TURKEY: 'Look, mate, this *is* my last Christmas –'

ME: 'You see, turkey, it's a dinner for a Christian occasion.'

TURKEY: 'Christian? I've seen you give bits to your bloody cat, is *he* Christian?'

ME: 'Well, I didn't want any to go to waste. . .'

TURKEY: 'All of me goes to waste, you know. On Boxing Day,

when you're slobbed out in the lounge, I'm floating down a London sewer.'

The time of the coming of the God-child is used in most foul ways – there's a perv in Soho who dresses up as Father Christmas, then solicits citizens: 'Merry Christmas – want to see a Christmas porn-film?'

And the unending plague of carol singers. One arrived at 11.30 p.m. on 1 December. I opened the door to a crowd of smiling-faced teenagers with a candle lantern. I couldn't resist it, I gave them a £1. It was only after they'd left I realized they were all Jewish and were collecting for the NSPCC – they had a good sense of timing, that's all. The next choir – I'd teach 'em. It soon came, angel voices. 'What do you bloody well want?' I shouted before I saw they were nuns. You can't win.

Will my father in distant Australia ever forget Christmas 1968 . . . my mother was dangerously ill. A devout Catholic, she asked for Communion every morning. My father (a lapsed Catholic) was told that the priest would arrive at 5.30 a.m. (before first Mass) and my father was to meet him at the door with a lighted candle, a bowl of water, and a towel. Now the priest had never set eyes on my father. Dead on 5.30 the door bell rang. My father, dressed in his best suit, opened the door. It was the local dustman, who eyed my father holding a candle, a bowl of water and a towel, and said, 'Don't worry, Mr Milligan, I've had a few rough nights myself. I dropped by to get the Christmas box.' My father, a bit thrown, said, 'Hold these,' and passed the candle, etc. while he went in to get some loose change, at which moment the priest arrives, sees the dustman (who was absolutely filthy) and says, 'Ah, good morning, Captain – you know, I never knew you were a dustman.' It broke my immaculate father's heart.

My own unforgettable Christmas was in 1956. I was living with my wife and two children in a rented crumbling Victorian home at Highgate. I loved my family, and had built up the children's belief in Father Christmas and how he came down the chimney. Now I was disappointed as a child at having heard my parents say; 'Just missed Father Christmas, he's just gone back up the chimney.' Well, my children wouldn't be denied that.

As fortune would have it, the chimney-breast was huge and still had the inlets for chimney-sweeps' boys to climb up. I decided my children would actually *see* Father Christmas, *and* coming down the chimney. I hired a Father Christmas costume, plus beard and wig. So on Christmas Eve I got up inside the chimney, hammered two nails inside and hung the pillowcase of presents there. On Christmas night it seemed the children would never sleep. Finally at midnight all was clear. I donned the costume wig and beard and, using mortician's wax, changed the shape of my nose. Carefully I climbed up the chimney, while the wife aroused the children with, 'Wake up – Father Christmas is coming,' and led them into the drawing-room.

Then disaster. I slipped and crashed with all the presents into the grate, bringing down a rain of soot; the nose bent, the beard came off. I got up in some pain to the children crying, 'Look Mummy, it's Daddy dressed up as Father Christmas.' Sod Christmas.

Nairobi Bus Depot, remarkable for its resemblance to Scunthorpe

Club International
Christmas Article

I am in Australia. I'm staying with my mother in a place called Woy Woy (woy it is called Woy Woy Ioy don't know). The old-fashioned wooden bush telephone rattles – it's a call from England! ('Hello sport – beaut call.' I say, it's my manager: 'Paul Raymond Publications *demand* you write, of all things, (wait for it) about the most unforgettable Christmas you had in the services during the war.' Well, I *could* conclude by saying *all* of them; I mean, it was wonderful! The Germans and us fired shells at each other with Goodwill and Love to All Men. Gunner White wrote on all shells 'Merry Christmas Friz', and when they got hit by that, it was the Last Noel. Oh yes! I remember sitting huddled in an OP and Lieutenant Walker listening for the distant carol-singing. 'O Tannenbaum, schoen Tannenbaum' would waft over from the German trenches and we would take a bearing on it with a holly-decorated prismatic compass, and then fire on them! Infantry sergeants would instruct their Bren gunners: 'Use yer red and green tracer tonight lads, it's more seasonal, looks like airborne 'olly, and *try* and not kill too many of them. Remember, it's Christmas.'

Ah yes! I remember those khaki Christmases. As to *the* most unforgettable, I'll have to try and remember it. There was the first one at Bexhill-on-Sea. Some of the Battery had been given leave, and on Christmas Eve 1940 I was in an OP at Galley Hill, Bexhill. It was very cold and the glass of the OP steamed up with the heat of my vibrant young porridge-and-lease-lend-bacon-filled body, being nourished by nips from a bottle of Johnnie Walker, a present from my parents, which arrived only three-quarters full as my father wanted to be sure it hadn't been 'watered'.

45

I peered out into the pitch black of the English Channel. The bastards! They were only 20 miles away. I imagined Adolf Hitler, stark naked, chasing Eva Braun with a sprig of mistletoe tied to his willy – 'Kom on mein darling – haff fun! It is Christmischer', and there was *me*, *alone*, skint, 3 fags, and 4 hours of duties. The telephone buzzed.

'World War II answering', I said.

There was a burst of stifled laughter from the other end, then a voice disguised as a ruptured Etonian said: 'Hell-o, who is that?'

'Gunner Milligan, sir. Trainee coward.'

Another burst of suppressed laughter. I daren't be rude in case it was an officer.

'Is everything all right?'

'All right? Haven't you heard? There's a war on. Er – who *is* that, sir?'

'The duty officer.'

'I don't recognize your voice, sir.'

'I've got a cold.'

'Yes, but who are you. . . sir?'

'It's Lieutenant Shag-a-dog-down-dead.'

A burst of hysterical laughter then he hung up. It rang again.

'Command Post – if that's Lieutenant Shag-a-dog-down-dead he can piss off.'

'How dare you. This is Captain Martin. Have you been drinking, Milligan? It's a serious offence when on duty.'

At which moment there was a terrific explosion from the minefield to the right. 'Was that you, Milligan?'

'No sir, I've never had it that bad, sir.'

'Well, what was it?'

'I don't know, sir, but I think it's pronounced B-A-N-G.'

'Go and see what it was, man. Hurry – my party starts in half an hour.'

'Yes, sir.'

I grab my Ross rifle and tin hat, and grope into the dark. How do you grope for a bang that's gone? I run down the hill – the grass in the minefield is on fire. I shine my torch – visions of catching German Paratroopers. Nothing. A policeman – I remember his name, Constable Nobbs – said: 'What happened, then?' (a Sussex accent).

'There was an explosion from there.' I pointed to the burning grass. 'I think a *mine* went off.'

He shone *his* torch. 'Now, you're a soldier, can a mine go orff on ees own?'

I knew the answer. 'No.'

'You sure?'

I knew the answer to that. 'No, I'm not.'

I hear the sound of a fire engine bell. As it approaches people open windows and shout 'Shhh.' A creaky, commandeered butcher's van is coming up the hill, pulling a portable fire appliance. Hooray! It's the Bexhill-on-Sea ARP Fire Brigade. Little old men, some still in their pyjamas, fall off it and start pulling a hose towards the burning grass. Just in time we stop them walking into a minefield. 'We'll have to use high pressure', says one who is doing nothing and is, therefore, in English law, in charge. But wait – 'Where's the nearest fire point?' he asks the policeman.

'There's nort one eere – nearest is Sea Road.'

'Our hoses won't reach that far – ahh.' The fire chief held one finger in the air – 'The sea! Get the suction end in the sea, lads.'

Two little men, their necks bent double under the weight of their steel helmets, throw their hose over the cliff. Clunk! The tide's out. 'Get down and pull it into the sea', shouts the fire chief, so two little men start a perilous journey after it. 'Hurry', shouted the leader, 'I think the fire's going out.' They hadn't had a good fire since the war started, their morale was 100 per cent filled with Churchill's speeches and this was their first chance for their 'finest hour'.

Well, this didn't last an hour, it started to rain. 'Quick, hold an umbrella over the fire', said the chief, but alas – the fire went out.

All that remained was for me to extricate the two little old ARP firemen now trapped on the cliff face. They were well and truly stuck. I shone my torch to ascertain their position, and they immediately shouted: 'Put that bloody light out, do you want the Bloody Germans to see us?' All attempts, including pulling them up on the hose, failed. The Constable takes charge: 'Have you a phone?'

I told him yes, and we trudge through the now squalling rain.

As we entered the OP a looming figure said: 'Are you the soldier on duty here?'

47

I assented.

'Why weren't you at your post?'

I explained, backed up by the Constable. 'I'm Lieutenant Mawson, Field Security. Why had you left your post?'

I explained the fire.

'Oh – I see,' he said.

'I must ask you the password, sir.'

'Niblet', he said.

I'm glad he knew it. I didn't. Sound of a midget voice played at high speed. My God, Captain Martin. I grab the phone.

'Where the hell have you been? I've missed six rounds waiting for you.' (Did he mean boxing or drinks.) I explained the story of the mine. 'The army, the police and the fire brigade were all present, sir – we saw no point in calling the navy.'

'Right. Well, be more careful in future', was his final command.

'Would you all like a nip of whisky?' I said to Lieutenant Mawson.

'Ah, well, just this once,' he said, swigging enough for twice. He passed it to the Constable.

'Cheers, a Merry Christmas.' He too took a giant, knee-crippling draught. In the dark it sounded like filling an empty bath tub from a great height. 'Ah', he gasped, having left enough in the bottle to cauterize a pimple.

A very wet ARP fire chief arrived. 'You 'aven't got a long piece of rope, have you lad? They are still stuck down the cliff.'

I patted my pockets. 'Sorry, I haven't got any long rope at all.'

'Oh dear,' he said. 'Mind if I sit down? I get these pains in my hip joints. I'm 66, you know.'

'No, I didn't know, but I'm glad you told me.'

'It's nice and warm in here – what is it?'

'It's me. I've got a temperature.'

To help him I phoned the gun position.

'What you want a long rope for at this bloody time of the night?'

'There's two firemen stuck down the cliff face.'

'Was the cliff on fire?'

'No,' I said. 'The cliff's not on fire, they were collecting gulls' eggs.' I explained the whole situation.

'Right, we'll send a coil.'

Lieutenant Mawson and the Constable left as soon as the bottle was empty. I was alone again. Finally a great three-ton lorry arrives with the coil of rope. What I report now is as told by Driver Wardle who delivered it.

The rain was getting heavier as they lowered the rope down the cliff. At first it missed, but after using a torch they located the two aged, white-faced terrors of the fire fiend. They were dragged up the cliff, moaning and groaning, finally reaching the top covered in clay, looking like Egyptian sunbaked mummies covered in glycerine. They didn't think it funny when Driver Wardle said: 'Merry Christmas, lads.'

Now! An old lady draws nigh. 'Is anyone in the Sentry Box?' she shouts.

'Yes. What is it madame? You know, this is a military area and civilians aren't allowed in.'

'I *am* a military', she says. 'My uncle is in the NAAFI. Are those men on the cliff looking for my dog?'

I told her no.

'Oh', she said. 'Do you mind if I come in and sit down, I get these pains in my hip joints. I'm 65, you know.'

'No, I didn't know.'

'It's nice and warm in here. What is it?'

'It's me, I've been drinking.'

'I wonder where my little darling is.'

At first I thought she had married a midget – it was the dog.

'His name is Hercules Brabazon-Brabazon – I named him after the painter.'

'He must have been thrilled to have a dog named after him.'

'He's been gone two hours.'

There was a pause as the penny dropped. 'Do you and your dog live near the minefield?'

'*Yes, right behind it*. When the Germans come we'll have a lovely view of them going up. I've put gran's chair near the window, she *is* looking forward to it.'

She left me just as my relief came in, Gunner Neat.

'You dirty bastard, screwing a woman on duty.'

'Give up . . . she's 65!'

'Loneliness can colour a man's mind.'

49

Neat was a man who wanted to believe things – for instance, if I had said my father had been run over by a steam roller and was now a book-marker in Lewisham Library, he'd believe it – he got some kind of kick out of it. After ten minutes of hotly denying his accusation, I finally said: 'OK, yes, I did screw her. I'll tell you for why – she pays you 2 quid for doing it.'

His jaw dropped open, his cigarette still sticking to his lower lip, revealing a set of rotten teeth that reminded me of Highgate Cemetery. 'Two quid,' he gasped. 'Two quid.'

'Of course – mind you – I've kept it secret . . . she lives behind the minefield.'

His evil mind was turning over. 'If I give you 5 borb [he was Cornish] would you do my turn?'

The money changed hands and he went out on his fool's errand.

I turned on the old Cossor wireless, held together with string and adhesive tape, and connected to our billet (a fisherman's cottage about 30 yards behind) by an electric cable. I remember, it was a broadcast from the Savoy Hotel; Carroll Gibbons and his Orpheans were playing a medley of Christmas songs and I could hear the cacophony of the half-cut dancers as they milled on the dance floor to the sounds of squeakers and odd balloons popping, lucky bastards! Why was *I* in a darkened OP alone with 5 shillings and an empty bottle of whisky. I lit up my last cigarette, it was 11.00. I wondered if Hitler had caught her yet.

Midnight came. The idiots at the Savoy all shouted and yelled meaningless sounds. The band played 'Should Auld Acquaintance' – it made me feel very lonely and neglected. The music continued. I drained the dregs of my whisky, about a tablespoonful, held it in my mouth as long as I could. Swilled it round my teeth, gargled with it, then drained it back in the bottle – one had to be economical. Anne Lenner is singing 'In Room 504 . . .' I must have dozed off. I awake to a smoke-filled OP. It was the wireless – I tried to beat out the flames with my balaclava, at the same time coughing like the dying Camille. The volume control went and the wireless roared out. Gingerly I carried it outside; the silence of the South Coast was shattered by Carroll Gibbons playing 'If I Wear a Little White Gardenia'.

The phone buzzes.

I answer: '*Cough – cough – cough – cough – cough – cough – cough – answer – cough – cough – cough – coughing.*'

'What's the matter, man?' It was the duty officer, Lieutenant Brewster.

'It's —*cough – cough – cough – phlegm – gasp – spit – cough* – it's the smoke – *cough – splutter – spit* – sir.'

'Then you must give them up . . . is everything all right?'

'*Cough – cough – cough – groan – gasp* – yes.'

'What?'

'I said – *cough – cough* – yes – *cough*'.

I take the phone outside before I asphyxiate. 'What's all that bloody noise?' he says.

'It's Carroll Gibbons and the Savoy Orpheans, sir.'

'Carroll Gibbons? Where?'

I wanted to say on the cliff. 'The wireless, sir.'

'Well, turn it down, man!'

'Pardon, sir?'

'I SAID TURN IT DOWN!'

'I CAN'T. IT'S ON FIRE!!'

'ARE YOU DRUNK, MILLIGAN?' he shrieked.

'JUST A MINUTE!!' There was one thing for it. I jumped up and down on the set until it died out. 'There'll be blue birds over . . .'

'I've switched it off, sir.'

'I should think so too. Anything to report? No? Goodnight and a Merry Christmas.'

Merry Christmas? One in the morning, no fags, no booze, no wireless, OP freezing!

Unbeknown to me, Neat *had* knocked on the old lady's door, said his piece, did his duty and was at this moment better off by £3. My joke had backfired. I could have done with that money. He told how next morning the death of the dog was told to the lady, though the news could have been broken to the lady less painfully. A policeman unwrapped a piece of newspaper revealing a blood-stained collar.

'Is this your dog?' he said.

A busy lunchtime at Mrs Thrills's boarding house

There and Backgammon

I always thought backgammon was a side of bacon – but seriously, folks. Dunhills have opted to hire the QE2 while it was going cheap; that is, floundering helplessly off Bermuda. It's a PR man's dream, a Transatlantic backgammon contest. They tell the Press. 'Sorry! there's no news value in gambling,' says Son of Beaverbrook, sticking 'FOR SALE' signs on his Rolls. 'I've only got one paper now, what we need are bigger names.' From the Dunhill boardroom the cry goes up: 'Get star names!'

At 3 in the morning they phoned Peter Sellers, who was in the Lotus position on the mantelpiece. 'PLEASEEE come,' whines a director from his coin-operated Bentley. 'I'll do my best,' says Peter. 'That's not good enough,' froths the Dunhill director. 'Look, there's a lot of rich old silver-haired ladies on board.'

'What are you trying to say?'

'I'm saying, bring *Milligan*, phone him now.'

'It won't be easy.'

'Why not?'

'He hasn't got a phone.'

'Don't stall, Sellers. We'll pay for the call.'

Peter does several more Lotus postures, a few 'Oms', half a bottle of Blue Nun and falls off. My phone rings at 4 a.m. 'Arghhh it's-a-lie-officer,-I-thought-she-was-under-16,' I say, arising from my Tryptazol-induced sleep.

'Peace on you,' coos Peter.

'. . . and peace on you too mate.'

'Look, Spike, you're getting on in life, you're 56, how'd you like to go to sea FREE, and meet some nice old ladies your own age? It won't cost you a penny. Now the good news, you don't have to tell jokes or wear a funny hat. I'll go if you go.' I grope in the dark for the light switch; the radio comes on. 'Do we travel first class or sewerage?'

'First.'

'One more thing, is Robin Day on board?'

'No.'

'OK. I'll come.'

The instructions from Jon Bradshaw are: 'Fly direct to New York, take a taxi to the docks, board the QE2 and come back.' A visa! I sent Tanis, my beloved Welsh hysterical receptionist, to the Embassy to a queue a mile long in which she is the only white person. We fill in the form she is given which demands answers from '*When, where, why and how were you born?*' to '*Which side do you dress during an Equinox?*' Every other question is '*ARE YOU A MEMBER OF THE COMMUNIST PARTY? HAVE YOU EVER SLEPT WITH A MEMBER OF THE COMMUNIST PARTY? DO YOU KNOW THE DIFFERENCE BETWEEN KARL AND GROUCHO MARX?*' We fill in all the gunge. Norma (my manager) trudges back to Grosvenor Square but, 'No, this is not good enough, madam.' *I* have to go in person. 'What's the trouble?' He points at the entry: *PLACE OF BIRTH* . . . India.

'It's insufficient evidence.'

'I'm standing in front of you, a position I could only have got to if I was born. Isn't that evidence?'

'We must have the town name.'

So. I fill in *PLACE*: Ahmednagar.

'Now,' I said. 'You know where India is on the map?'

'Yes.'

'Do you know where Ahmednagar is?'

'No.'

'You see, now you're bloody lost. You should have settled for India.'

I was to return the next day for the visa (ha, ha, ha, ha).

Third day of the great visa story: 'What's bloody wrong now?'

'Its about your mental condition. In the form against *ANY SERIOUS MENTAL ILLNESS?* you have put: ¿No.'

'So?'

'I saw you on the David Dimbleby TV show in which you appeared to be in a manic depressive state.'

54

'Of course I was! They only gave me 3 quid for the show.'

'But that condition must be serious.'

'Look, if I was seriously mentally ill – do you think I'd be appearing on BBC television? My God, it takes enough trouble getting them to accept *sane* people.'

'I'm sorry! We need to see a doctor's certificate.'

'Look, mister, if it's Richard Nixon you're worried about, the CIA will get him long before I do. If you're not careful I won't go to America.'

I go to my physican, the immaculate, precise, intelligent Richard Bell, show him the latest form. (a) *Have any of your parents ever tried to assassinate anyone?* (b) *How many times have you seen 'Hair'?* (c) *Are you related to Jack Ruby?* (d) *If you were given the opportunity, who would you kill first: President Nixon/Ronald Reagan?* (e) *What time?* (f) *Do you like the United States Marines or Doris Day?* (g) *Did you ever touch Lenny Bruce?*

'I don't think', said Richard, 'they will be satisfied with anything less than Spike Milligan is a self-confessed psychopathic homosexual with homicidal paranoia.' Richard dictates a lengthy report on my mental condition. 'Mr Spike Milligan has had one nervous breakdown in 1956, he was given Medinal, he is now recovered, etc. etc.'

'It's still not good enough,' says an officious Yankee female in Booth B. 'We must know how many milligrams of the drug, how many times a day, etc. etc.!' and walked away like she was the risen Christ. Well, it was goodbye to her. I phoned the Ambassador.

'He's not here, he's in the USA.'

'Oh, and his deputy?'

'He's on holiday.'

'You know what happened to Israel when they went on holiday?'

'Pardon?'

'Who is looking after the shop? I mean, if the Russians' atom bomb dropped on Grosvenor Square, who is in charge?'

'Oh. There's an aide.'

'Give me him.'

A nice man gets on. I explained all the crapology that's going on and he solves the problem from the top. Come round tomorrow and you'll have the visa. So sucks to Booth B madonna, and I sent off a secret donation to the Wounded Knee Legal Fund.

THE FLIGHT INTO THE AMERICAS

16 APRIL: my Birthday, Charlie Chaplin's birthday, Hitler's birthday. I'm picked up by a mini-cab, a lovely sunny day, not too much traffic on the road, we crash into the back of a car. Happy Birthday. The two drivers are slanging each other as the clock ticks dangerously towards take-off. I intervene and get set on by both of them. I transfer to a taxi, and leave them hitting each other. At Heathrow I get a telegram from Sellers. 'Sorry, can't make the trip. Have to to buy a new car on Doctor's orders.' The swine. I'm wafted to the VIP lounge which is full of the very opposite.

I get a window seat on the Jumbo. I'm joined by Hon. Michael Pearson.

'Peter's not coming,' he said. 'His Guru told him he had a sense of impending doom.'

'Whose?'

'Ours.'

'Two brandies, please.'

There is a disparity about our time of arrival:

British Airways, London: 'You'll arrive at 3.30, Sir.'

Stewardess: 'You'll arrive at 2.15, Sir.'

Captain: 'You'll arrive at . . . 4.00, Sir.'

Finally, the Captain announces: 'Hello, etc. We are half an hour ahead of schedule, we will therefore be landing at two o'clock.' Ten minutes later – 'Sorry that should have been one o'clock because of the hour difference in Summer Time.' We land at thirteen minutes past one. The ship doesn't sail till eight. We hire a cab and drop our luggage at the docks which appear to be in desperate need of a government grant.

'Nobody gits on board until after five,' says a man like Schnozzle Durante.

We mooch around New York, and in 4 hours see enough to wean me off it for life. I phone Peter Cook, 'What are you doing in New York, you naughty fellow?'

'There's a traffic jam at Marble Arch, I detoured.'

At 5 o'clock I am ascending the QE2 gang-plank. A man at the top puts a crappy pink Lei around my neck – 'Welcome to the QE2.'

'You're welcome to it, too,' I say. The cabin is a replica of every modern hotel room built since 1950, and I'm looking for the signature of Richard Seifert. The room is sterile and gives all the glamour of travelling by hospital ward. In my head it's GMT midnight, so I went to bed. So when the Queen sailed and the decks were crammed with romantic fools I was ninny byes. I arose at dawn to catch the sunrise. It spilled blood-red lights on to the sleepless sea. I ran around the deserted decks. A lone insomniac appeared.

'Nice day for a sail,' he coughed.

'Yes, let me know if you see one,' I said, side-stepping him.

The ship's rubbish is getting tipped into the Atlantic. I return sweating to my cabin and gasp to the Cabin Steward.

'Brian, for God's sake open the porthole.'

'Don't you like air conditioning, Sir?' he says.

'Love it, but outside there's the real thing.'

'Is there? Cor fancy that!' he said, and opened it.

I ordered tea and toast, delicious. Arghhhh! The Muzak has started. I turn the knobs to get a classical channel. Ah! Tchaikovsky's *Nutcracker*, plus BBC Overseas News. I wrestle to another channel: Mantovani. OK. The next 10 minutes is spent rushing back and forth to control a volume that goes from complete silence to ear-shattering. The passenger list. My God, Sir Seymour Edgerton, my bank manager, is on board. Where can I hide? I must find a ragged suit and a begging bowl. The old office of Purser has gone now, it's Hotel Manager, so this is not a ship it's a hotel. What's wrong with being a ship?

'No sir, that is not a life boat, that is a survival room.' My writing is interrupted. Grafted over Barbra Streisand singing *People* is the voice: 'Hello, this is the Captain speaking. I'm sorry to say that repairs to the boilers are still going on, and I'm sorry to say that we are under reduced power, we are only making 23 knots (well tie 'em faster damn 'ee) and I'm sorry to say PEOPLE WHO LIKE PEOPLE ARE THE we will be, I'm sorry to say, some hours late in arriving at the LUCKIEST PEOPLE IN THE WORLD thank you.' This is the end. Using my breakfast knife, I disconnect the entire communications system and at last I can hear the sea! A swim. The brochure says Heated Pool. I plunge in, the water is freezing. I claw my way out with Angina. 'It's–it's freezing,' I tell the attendant lady. 'Yes, it is,' she grinned. 'Why didn't you tell me?' 'You didn't ask.' I risk going on deck and mixing with the peasants. A ravishing blonde smothered in bosoms approaches, giggles, and says, 'Here, weren't you Spike Milligan?' 'Yes, I weren't,' I said. 'Shouldn't you be in the milking shed?' Several more asinine encounters drive me to the ship's library. I borrow *The Exorcist*, and end up that night under the bed screaming, 'I am possessed by an evil Protestant 2nd Engineer.'

Punch have asked me to 'Look in and report on the backgammon.' I follow the sound of rattling dice and arrive at a room deep in sporting gloom. I sidle up to contestant Hon. Michael Pearson. 'How's it going, Michael?' 'Piss off,' he says. He was losing.

The tables are alive with Dunhills sporting flags, matches and ashtrays, everything but fags. A film crew are at work. 'Look,' says the producer, 'what we need, Spike, is something to funny the film up.'

'Really,' I said. 'There's a very funny man on the ship.'

'Who is he?'

'The Captain.'

I'm bored and return to my cabin. The phone is ringing. 'Spike, this is Clement Freud, how about lunch?'

'I'm sorry, I haven't got any on me.'

'I'll nip down to your cabin and pick you up.'

'I'm heavy.'

Clement takes me to the Grill Room. He's not happy with the cuisine and referring to the mayonnaise, says: 'My compliments to the chef and tell him yuck.'

INCIDENT FOR THE INCREASE OF BLOOD PRESSURE

ME *(on the phone to the Bureau):* 'Hello, is that the Bureau?'

SWEET TWITTERING FEMALE: 'Yes.'

ME: 'Is it possible to send out a call on your intercom for Mr Quentin Crisp to come to the phone?'

SWEET: 'Are you a passenger?'
ME: 'No, I'm swimming alongside.'
SWEET: 'Is it an emergency?'
ME: 'Yes, he owes me money.'
I give up. I return to writing this article.

17, 18, 19 APRIL: The backgammon game goes on in a great burst of indifference daily; the ship's paper reports the casualties. CLEMENT FREUD ELIMINATED. THE HON. MIKE PEARSON DEFEATED AND CRYING IN HIS CABIN.

Now the bad news. I suddenly run a temperature and am confined to my cabin. 'I want you to keep travellers' cheques handy,' says the ship's doctor.

'What have I got?'

'You've got a temperature. That will be five guineas.'

So pass the 20th and 21st.

The ship has developed a heavy roll, which they give me for breakfast. Brian, my cabin steward, is a hero. 'Anything you want sir, just press the button, and if I hear it I'll come.'

A backgammon shudder runs through the ship. Victor Lowndes has been eliminated and is selling copies of *Playboy* in the galley.

Sunday 21st: Still groggy in bed. How can you get malaria on the QE2? Perhaps the doctor's wrong. 'Did you have it in the war?' he said, feeling in my pockets for money.

'Well, yes.'

'Ah, then it's come back.'

'After 30 years?'

'The bug has a strong dormancy factor.'

'What's that mean?'

'Another five guineas. Try and keep it going till tomorrow,' he says. And exits.

Tonight the finals of the backgammon – Barclay Cooke (US) vs. Charles Benson (GB), who has been doing the boots at night to keep himself going. The prize: £10,000. After paying his bar bill and tipping the stewards that should leave him with about £2.50.

The form-filling lunacy goes on unchecked. I have written my name, date of birth, etc. 25 times, each piece of information identical to the previous form. Who gets these bloody things? I fill

59

one up to get on the plane, I fill one up to get off the plane. I fill one in for the US Immigration authorities, one for the US Customs authorities, I fill one up to get on the boat, I fill another three up while I'm at sea, now I'm filling them up to get off the boat, to give to the Immigration Officers; the Cunard Registration Form, the English Customs Declaration Form. It is a great piece of bureaucratic repetition. I mean, their files must be groaning with my forms, I've been filling them in for the past 30 years. What do they do with them? Why do they need them? Each time I fill the form in I'm still the same person, with the same date of birth. Don't these silly bastards know there is a paper shortage, and an energy shortage, mostly mine? Feel better after that. Now let's see who's won the contest.

Very, very strange. The ship's paper *ignores* the finals and makes absolutely no mention of who the winner is, but the lavatory attendant tell me it's Mr Charles Benson of England! Thank God it's all over. Barclays Bank have run out of sterling, and Cherbourg is off the port bow! Landdddd! the grateful cry goes up.

The last day. Cherbourg: we can have 3 hours ashore. Barclays Bank has specially closed down so we can't get francs. It's half a mile to the town, no transport. I walk. The pay-off? It's early closing in Cherbourg. Dying for the loo, I find one, am stopped by the Madame.

'M'sieur,' she waves 3 pieces of toilet paper at me, '*Dix francs*.' I only have sterling; have you ever had the indignity of handing back 3 pieces of toilet paper? Back to the ship. With a bursting bladder, I give a watery farewell to France.

Tomorrow England, Home and Mortgage! The corridors are turning into great luggage dumps. 'Did you know two out of three baggage stewards are ruptured?' said a groaning porter. Dawn! Men from Her Majesty's Everything see that you are out of your bed early enough to be unhappy, they collect the bits of paper, and leave. Charles Benson comes down the gangplank, his cases stuffed with money.

Standing at the dockside, his pyjamas showing below his trousers, is the *Punch* courier. 'Have you got it?' I hand him the article. The voyage is over. Where's the telly? It's a good ship.

Two of Mrs Thrills's lady guests
convalescing from lunch

My Day

They want me to write a thousand words called *My Day*. This title seems to have onerous connotations of blue-rinsed elderly ladies writing on dove pink notepaper eating a marshmallow with the left hand and feeding chicken vol-au-vent to an aging myopic Pekinese in whose veins runs the blood of the Tang Emperors. I really cannot write a compact *My Day* because my day never finished. It started on 16 April 1918 in a wooden military maternity hospital at Ahmednagar and the bloody thing has been going on ever since. However, I will impart to you a section of this day.

It seems that in high establishment authoritative areas I am described as 'Very unpredictable and unreliable', so I will start by saying I wake up unpredictably and unreliably on the stroke of 7 a.m., I go unpredictably and unreliably to the bathroom and there, unpredictably and unreliably, have a shower. I then shampoo my hair (unpredictably and unreliably, of course). Having completed that I turn the water to cold and stick it as long as I can – my record for living under a 2 degrees below freezing shower is .348 of a second. This, of course, is accompanied by screams (mine). I then take a coarse white towel with a heavy weave (Harrods 28 gns per square inch) and try and stimulate a glowing warmth to my skin, which is still brown from my unreliable and unpredictable trip to Australia.

The next move could be divided into two. If I have slept at the office overnight I drink a glass of fresh orange juice from a fresh tin. If I am at home I ask our darling Nanna to make me some toast from wholemeal bread, some honey from bees that have culled their honey from real flowers, and this along with a cup of Earl Grey tea is my breakfast.

I then go downstairs and wrestle with Fred Flora McDonald, a small female West Highland terrier, for possession of the remains of the morning papers, starting with the *Morning Star* and terminating with *The Times*. I then become aware of the unreliability of the English Press – for instance, a simple occasion like Prince Charles' twenty-first birthday was covered thus:

Daily Telegraph	Prince Charles the Heir Apparent is 21 today
Private Eye	The Apparent Heir is 21 today
Financial Times	The FT index shows that Prince Charles is 21.3 years old today
Morning Star	Prince Charles is 21 today on the backs of the workers
and finally *The Times*	According to our Correspondent Prince Charles was 21 yesterday

With these staggering variations on a theme, I then take a canvas zip bag and stuff into it various telephone books, bits of paper, drawings and paintings done by my children, sayings, ideas that have occurred to me, notes to buy bird food for the garden, notes reminding me that three windows have been broken and need repairing, notes that the famed GPO telephone by my bed is not working yet again, notes reminding me that my brand-new Mini Clubman has screws falling out all over the place, that the right-hand door will not open, and that the only accesss is through the boot, a reminder to write to the Caretaker of the Herbert Samuel Hall who, because I parked my car behind the hall, let all four tyres down and stuck labels on the windscreen.

The time is now, say, 8.30 a.m. I then drive to the office at Orme Court, Bayswater, avoiding what I call 'The Sheep Run', that is, Golders Green and West End Lane. I haul around the back streets past Hendon Football Club, enjoying on the way the last two cottages standing from the Old Brent Farm. I follow the old

Clitterhouse Lane, at the same time listening to early morning classics on whatever band the BBC are putting it out, hoping it will be Delius – or Satie. On the dashboard of the car I have a pad and pencil on which I jot down ideas for lyrics for some songs I have written, which George Martin is pressing me to finish for an LP I am doing. Three miles from home I pass the Clitterhouse Lane Farmhouse and remind myself to write to Lady Dartmouth at the GLC Historic Buildings Division to have a look at it, and consider it unique in that it is the last complete farm in North London still surviving, though, alas, not as a going concern. I keep a constant look-out for buildings that might need saving.

On one such occasion I stop outside a titanic early Victorian house in Kilburn; I see that it has the sign 'Acquired' outside, which shows the devious methods with which the house has been obtained by a Buyer. I take a torch, I enter the place and, of course, it is vandalized from top to bottom. I try to fit together the story of the people who lived there by their sombre remains. This means maybe two hours of going through letters strewn around, a school report dated 1905, the 1912 prescription for Dr Collis' linctus 'Good for the 'flu' written on it in spidery handwriting, and in my mind the whole house gradually comes alive. I see the ghosts on the staircase, I see the now fractured early imitation Spode soup plates lying divided on the floor. I strip off the wallpaper to see what the original one was like and take a small sample, bearing in mind to show it to the Finchley Society, of which I am President.

I arrive at the office maybe about 10 a.m. On this day in particular I had received a Braille letter from a girl I befriended; her name was Martine Burton. I make a note to send her a taped message from me, which she can play on her Philips cassette recorder which I managed to get Philips to give to her free, likewise a small portable radio which brought a great amount of pleasure into her life and which makes me feel very, very good.

Among the mail, of course, there are many cries for help from neurotics, would-be writers, painters, preservation societies – all of which takes well up into two in the afternoon. Lunch for me just does not exist – it is cups of tea during the day, and a non-fattening biscuit which I am sure is made of concentrated sawdust held together with gum arabic. The floor of my office is littered with stray teeth resulting from contact with these strange inedible substances. I contact my wife and find she is with Lady Dowding planning another campaign against the slaughter of seal pups in Canada.

I am now somewhere in the middle of the Jimmy Young Show and wondering with bated breath who that woman is who makes a telephone call to him every day using a different voice each time. I am unable to believe it when Jimmy says 'Who is that speaking?' and a very high, constricted voice says 'Mrs Eileen Nasty of Bullocks Drive, Clacker in Beds.' I realize, no matter how great a comedy writer I might become, I could never invent names as funny as that. I listen for the recipe and realize that one spoonful of it could mean instant death, so I switch to the BBC operatic channel where painful castrati tenors are holding their rupture appliances and squeezing out top Cs, which obviously is going to ruin their sex life. Peter Sellers phones me from Dublin – he feels a bit down, Miranda his wife has been ill. We chat, and cheer each other up. I remember to write to Prince Philip thanking him for his telegram he sent on the occasion of breaking an Art Gallery window. His telegram said 'Good Shot'. I think he's a good bloke.

Next comes the time-consuming chore of arguing with insurance brokers about the accident I had, telephoning the Inland Revenue and trying to make them understand I am worried because my tax is five years behind, to which I get the reply: 'I am very sorry but I have only just got the file because your accountant has changed his address.' That apparently is sufficient explanation. I ask him a straight question: 'How much surtax do I pay for 1965?' HE CANNOT ANSWER. I contact Alun Owen in Eire and ask him what the advantages would be if I became domiciled in Dublin. 'None,' he says. 'What you save you spend on drink.'

Of course, all this time one is combatting the GPO telephone system. My office telephones are marvellous – I dial my home on one and I get a click. I discover that you have to pick up the second telephone and dial again and then you get the number, and I don't know whether to laugh or cry. Usually I do both, and holding up a photograph of the Minister in question I roll it slowly into a crumpled ball, set fire to it, then dance on it in my bare feet. My daughter Laura phones me – I tell her I have booked for the whole family to see *Godspell* at the Round House, and 'Oh yes, I'm getting engaged.' Help! I am aware now that the pigeons at the back of my office are awaiting their daily feed of Swoop, which I extend to them in five handfuls. I recognize the two young pigeons who were hatched in May 1971.

A letter from my mother in Australia tells me: 'It has been pouring torrents of rain for two days. I don't mind as it is good for the garden and I do my sewing in that time.'

I plug in my electric kettle and when boiling make myself possibly the fifth cup of tea in three hours. I use Earl Grey, no milk, only lemon – taken me forty-five years to learn how to make tea properly.

I read through the monthly journals of the Animals' Defender, of which I am a supporter. I read with pleasure that two MPs, Richard Boddy and Kenneth Lomas, are both actively fighting to bring about some humane conditions for animals, who suffer grievous pain, 5,000,000 of them being experimented upon a year. A letter from André Previn, thanking me for a poem I dedicated to him.

André Previn
   Went to Heaven
But was a mite too soon
   St Peter said
'You are not quite dead
   'Come back this afternoon.'

The BBC news is now telling me of the tense condition in Rhodesia, and we realize that the police state is still firmly entrenched, and that liberty for our coloured brothers is a long way off, and I think, like Che Guevara thought, that there are times when liberty can only be brought about by 'shooting those that suppress it'. A sad thought but true. I am in the middle of writing a half-hour TV show for BBC. Phones are going.

I make a note to contact Bill Evans, the American jazz pianist, to take him to dinner, to tell him how much I appreciate his piano playing and that it was destroyed for me at Ronnie Scott's by a bass player who took solos the whole time and clouded the sensitive playing of Evans. I telephone my secretary and ask her to buy a pair of boxing gloves, which I will send to the bass player and ask him could he wear them during Bill Evans's solos?

In the post I received four tickets for the England–Ireland Rugby match in Paris for 29 January and I decide it would be madness to go to Paris and not have dinner there, so I try to get through to the French Tourist Agency to book a meal on the *bateaux mouche*.

I telephone my publisher and say to him:

ME: 'Good morning. Can I speak to Raleigh Trevelian?'

RALEIGH: 'Good morning, Spike.'

ME: 'Isn't it a lovely morning, it is almost like spring – I feel crocuses growing in my head. Raleigh, I have been writing serious poems for some years, going back to the War, and they were very amateurish to begin with but I have improved considerably. This does not mean I am good, just that I have improved. Would you consider reading them and publishing them? But do tell me the truth – if you think they are too trivial please say so.'

RALEIGH: 'Of course.'

I am so overjoyed at the thought of being accepted that I cannot resist reading my latest one over the telephone to him.

Metropolis

I see barbaric sodium city lamps
pretending they can see.
They make a new mad darkness.
Beyond their orange pools
the black endlessness of time.
What, in that unseen dark tomorrow is waiting. . . .
That iron tomorrow coming on unknown wheels
Who is the driver,
Will he see me in time?

Woy Woy, NSW
October 1971

67

I realize that the number of poems are so small that it will make a very slender volume indeed, so I decide to ask my daughter Laura would she like to do some designs and illustrate the poems. As Laura lives in her own mews flat with no telephone and is at Art School all day, trying to contact her is rather like trying to get to the moon on a tricycle. I leave a message with Benny, her boyfriend, who works on 'the vans', and I am still waiting for a reply.

I seem to have written a thousand words and still have not got through the day.

Add to the above 100 telephone calls, 50 letters, form filling and pushing the ever unproductive English workman to do jobs he promised to do and never will.

Around about nine at night I decide to stop all the nonsense and I usually make my way to Ronnie Scott's, sit in a dark corner, order a bottle of Moselle, listen to the jazz, and about 12.45 I leave – go back to the office – read a few scripts – sleep.

Help! I've forgotten to book air seats to Paris for the England–Ireland match.

HELP!

Holidaymakers being evacuated on board a hospital ship after two weeks at Mrs Thrills's boarding house

Un homme libre dans la rue
à Scunthorpe

One Man's Week

Monday Arise at 7.30. Open the window and scream. Put telephone back on hook. London Broadcasting, where news comes first (also second, third, fourth and fifth), is telling us the latest. 'Belfast 3 bomb explosions, London 2. Belfast still lead by 311. . . the news is all bad, but does the announcer have to sound as if he is personally involved in it? Even the most trivial news is read in a hard-driving the-world-is-ending-tomorrow-voice, i.e. 'Today the Queen Mother opened a Flower Show at Bournemouth', but when he says it, you feel as though the Queen Mother has broken into a Bournemouth flower shop wearing a stocking mask and shot the proprietor.

Why, why, why do they all create an atmosphere of tension? Likewise sports reports: 'Manchester United smashed to defeat today etc. etc. Leeds pulverize Villa in savage 5-goal attack. Tottenham destroyed in 3 devastating minutes.' We complain about soccer hooliganism, yet all the matches are described in violent terms . . . The news continues. Moslems and Christians are slaughtering each other in . . . Basques and Spaniards . . . In Ulster Protestants and Catholics . . . Portugal Left against Right on the verge of Civil War. . . . I suppose what it all boils down to is man's never really quite happy unless he's killing himself. And it's still only Monday.

Another Day I've got to go to the Prince of Wales (Theatre), a post-show presentation to Harry Secombe. I go backstage in the interval – we have a laugh. After the show it was intended that Peter Sellers, Michael Bentine and I were to give Secombe the Variety Club award for his one-hundreth year in show business.

Alas, Bentine is confined to bed with a severe overdraft, and Sellers is in America studying the plans of his next wife, so I have to clod on the stage at the end and say: 'Harry Seacrune, apparently you haven't been found out yet, so on behalf of someone or other here is something or other Value £2.50 VAT 37p.' He then looked at me and said 'Who is this man? The play isn't over yet. Throw him in the general direction of out.' It was a thick first-night audience. One had the feeling that once they had established they could afford the £25 seat, they left. Back in his dressing-room, Secombe consumes so much brandy that he convinces me he has weaned himself off food.

Monday continues   The story of man's follies continues. An Air India flight arrives at Heathrow. From it step one hundred well fed, well tanked up, tired but healthy people – 'Air India looks after you.' In the hold of the plane are 171 little dead birds; in two following flights the number of dead birds total 2,000. I phone Mr Whitaker, the Manager, RSPCA Heathrow. Like me, he is morally decimated at the needless killing of these small creatures. I ask him who's responsible; they won't tell him. He does, however, find the name of one home importer, and I print their name large: LADY DELL of Worthing. I write to Fred Peart, Minister of Agriculture, and ask him does he intend putting an end to this outrageous trade. If so, what? I have my hackles up and I decide to do something positive. To my way of thinking a law that imposed massive fines on airlines would stop the trade dead in its tracks. With that in mind I write to people asking them to become patrons of my cause. I write to Prince Charles and say if he becomes *the* Patron, I will let him off the hook for fox hunting. Lady Dowding promises support, so does Michael Foot . . . Good heavens, it's still Monday!

Monday   I watch a bureaucratic charade on TV. The Hounslow Council have spoken. Women's Aid under Erin Pizzey are the only organization who give immediate safe refuge to Battered Wives and Children. Needless to say, they are overcrowded. 'Unless you evict half the women and children, we will withhold our financial aid.' The reason is there is a health and fire hazard. The latest inmate, Mrs Gwen X (I can't print her name for fear of reprisals by

71

her husband) arrived with six broken ribs, a swollen face, and scalds between her thighs – and all done by her husband in full view of their six-year-old little girl. Alderman A. King says: 'If they go to their local social worker they will help.' Well, we then see Mrs Gwen X who had gone to her social worker who told her: 'Go back to your husband.'

I cannot see the reasoning of the Hounslow Council. I decided to help. We will put on a Poetry and Jazz Concert on Sunday 2 November at 8.30 p.m. at Ronnie Scott's, who has given the hall free for Women's Aid. Sir Bernard Miles says: 'Of course I'll do something, Spike.' Likewise Christopher Logue, Bill Kerr, the Stan Tracey Quartet. There's no shortage of volunteers . . . This wife-battering is a terrible thing. I wish I could do more.

Still Monday, Bloody Monday   I am thinking about the Blackpool Conference. Old hat by the time you read this, but the aftermath still lingers on. What I thought was a monumental piece of walking backwards was the rejection of the chance of Electoral Reform. OK, it's democracy, but the *reason* for rejecting it, to quote the prime mover against, Mr Angus Maude, was: 'Why should we make it possible to let in another 100 Liberals, when the most they can ever muster is 20?' My God, the nerve!!! He's not interested in the electorate, only the fear of letting in Liberals!!! He concluded with: 'Why should we have Electoral Reform when we have no idea of the consequences?' Thank God Jenner didn't think like that, or the entire Conservative Party would be pox-marked.

My God, It's Still Monday   I'm rehearsing my new TV series, Q6 (why Q6? Why not?). We have an hour to go to recording time and we have a disaster. One of the sketches is about a Day in the Life of an Ordinary Pakistani Dalek (eh?), in which we use the original Daleks, but NO! The agent for the copyright refuses to let us 'make fun of the Daleks'. What to do? I phone the inventor, Terry Nation. He's heard about the trouble and says: 'Listen Spike, I've been waiting to repay a favour. Remember when I first came to London 23 years ago, broke, you lent me 20 quid to tide me over?'

'Did you pay it back?'

'No.'

'Well, the interest on that will keep me for life.'

'Listen. I'll let you use the Daleks and we'll call it square.'

'OK.'

It is the last show of the series, so I take the entire cast and technical crew to the Kalamaris Restaurant. I awake next morning face downwards on the office floor fully clothed. What went wrong? Curse, it's Monday again.

Monday   Midday Concert for the women of Holloway Prison. I can't understand – you can only give them one and a half hours' entertainment. If I had gone over time, would they have let me out?

The fourth Monday in a row, it's got to stop.

My continuing battle with food additives is reagitated by a sticker on a packet of jam tarts: 'These tarts *must* be eaten before 7 November.' Why? What exactly happens to them on the 8th? I mean, if you put them in the fridge and forget to eat them before the 9th, when you open the fridge does a green hairy arm covered in jam reach out and pull you in? I can't believe that man has got to the state where he is swallowing millions of tons of chemical additives a year, and has never ever been asked if he agreed to them being put in his food. Who's in charge?

The Last Monday   The end of the week, and one thing looms large in my mind. Someone is spending a lot of money on publicity for Mrs Thatcher . . . . Who?

Yet another Monday, 19 October. To dinner at Michael Foot's home. When I entered the room Tom Driberg stood up. Has my time come at last? On my left hand was Paul Foot. Had a wonderful dinner, which terminated with the table opening in two, and those at each end having to keep their knees at 14 ins above normal to keep the table stable for the cheese and biscuits. Yes, Michael is a great man, so am I, so is Tom Driberg, so is Paul Foot, and so is Mrs Jill Foot. It took 18 bottles to reach that stage. Take a little wine for thy stomach's sake – well, I also took it for my legs, arms, teeth, ankles and the abdominal ridge.

I must fly now, I feel an attack of British Railways coming on.

Mrs Thrills reading the morning obituary notices

Sykes and Golf

Eric Sykes is a famous human being, and in his dying years has taken up the game of golf. He uses the clubs more as a support to help him round the course, and for each teeing shot he has to receive 400 grammes of gum arabic in a hypodermic to supply energy for the drive. He is the inventor of the amazing vacuum golf club. The club head for this invention is fitted with a small door on the lead face. When you hit the ball it disappears into the club head, but has given the appearance of a tremendous drive out of sight. The trick is then to approach the ground, standing 3 ins from the hole, and press the release button which ejects the concealed ball from the golf club head to hole in 2. Watch out for this point during the game. It is a new interesting phenomenon in the world of golf.

I wish him well in the game. Everybody wishes him well in the game. It is a pity he keeps losing.

Peter Sellers and Spike Milligan, finalists in the Brass Band Contest
(Economy Section) – Scunthorpe Municipal Baths

The Hell of Flying

There was a time when Canopus and Solent flying boats, complete with beds, cabins, lounges etc., would fly one to Australia, but – ha ha – since then we've made that bloody pardon-me-howling-with-laughter-word 'Progress'. Let me recount that progress, if at all, amounts to 300 mph faster, and 20,000 feet higher; the rest is sheer agony. When I pay BA or Qantas or South African or TWA airlines hundreds and hundreds of pounds to travel first class, the word 'first' should have a meaning beyond more grog, grovelling and grub. One needs most of all on a long journey to, say, Australia, relaxation, tranquillity and rest – and do we get it? My God we don't! Let me carry out a blow-by-blow account of the punishment from the moment we board.

First that terrible sound-swill is playing, that unbearable Muzak. Even more terrible, the sound control is with, not a musician or a passenger, but a member of the cabin staff, and the degree of blasting you get depends on exactly how thick or deaf he is. He has no idea what is on the Musak tape – one is fed absolute absurdities. Board a BA 747 on a snow-bound day at Heathrow, and the idiot machine will be playing 'Springtime in Vienna'. It is mindless. No one listens to it. It is a waste of time. money and energy and is IM-POSED upon the traveller irrespective of whether he wants it or not.

I show my boarding pass to a young thing who by her slightly dazed reaction shows she has not been on the plane much longer than I have. 'Now see, in a Trident the As are there and on a 747 there.' She shows me my seat.

'I asked for, and was told, I would be in a non-smoking area. This is a smoker.'

'Oh, we'll see what we can do after we take off,' she says.

Great, I wish I could say that when I was buying my ticket: 'I'll see what I can do about paying you.'

'Paper, sir,' says a sweet young thing.

'Yes, I'd like the *Guardian*.'

'Sorry, there's only the *Financial Times* and the *Sun*.' I see, it's money or tits. I opt for the money rag. As I'm excitedly reading about the variability of the equity market, I am offered a glass of champagne.

'No, thanks. I don't drink at 10.30 of a morning.'

'Orange juice?'

'No, thanks. I had some for breakfast.'

All my answers are received with a commutability. It's either yes or no and, like the milkman's horse, she moves on at the word 'no'. All the other regular travelling slobs are downing the stuff so they can forget who they are. I'm looking for some news in the *Financial* –

'Canapés before lunch, sir?'

'It's a bit early for lunch.'

'Oh, it's not yet.'

'When?'

'As soon as we take off.'

'When is that?'

'There's been a delay so we can't say.' (Note the Royal We.)

'No lunch for me then.'

The word 'no' sends her on her way. I am looking for news in the *Financial Ti* –

'Writing paper and post cards, sir?'

I accept them. I note the smoking lunatics are clenching and unclenching their fists waiting for the NO SMOKING signs to disappear. Some of the loonies are sitting with a cigarette in their mouth, match in one hand and matchbox in the other. The Muzak grinds endlessly on. I am looking for news in the *Financial Ti* –

'Headphones, sir.'

'What for.'

'The music channels, sir.'

'Music? I can hear it playing quite clearly.'

'No. These are other music channels.'

'I'll think about it.'

'It's one pound for the headset.'

I am looking for news in the *Financial Ti* –

'Programme, sir.'

'What for?'

'The music channel.' She sticks it in my hand.

I am looking for news in the *Financial Ti* –

'Hot towels?'

'No, thank you. I can't eat another thing.'

I am looking –

'Socks and eye masks?'

I'm handed another envelope with the stuff in. When in Christ is it going to stop? Almost immediately I am given the lunch menu. A bowl of peanuts is put beside me (YOU'VE GOT TO HAVE THEM).

'More champagne, sir?'

I have given up trying to read. I sit back, look blankly ahead, listening to the Muzak gunge pour out.

An announcement: 'Will cabin crew check all doors for take-off.'

Hooray, that actually stopped the Muzak. Wait. No, it's back again.

Announcement: 'Good morning, this is your captain speaking. I'm sorry about this delay, it's to do with the rain, but we should be taking off shortly.' Muzak.

'Will you fasten your safety belt, please.'

Ah! the Muzak has stopped. 'Hello, hello. Ladies and gentlemen, under your seat you will find a life jacket. In the event of an emergency, etc. etc.' The girl stewardess does the cabaret, and we all cheer at the end. Muzak.

Hoping that the interruptions are over, I start to read *Twenty-four Hours in Entebbe*, and wish I was there and not on this bloody plane.

'This is your flight deck steward. For your information, the stewards or stewardesses [and there's very little difference] can be called by pulling the button in your arm rest. Thank you.'

We're moving!!

'Hello, ladies and gentlemen, this is your captain speaking.

We've had a clear for take-off, so we should be airborne in about 12 minutes. Thank you.'

There is hardly a pinpoint between the announcement and the interruptions. You realize we are all on one great conveyor belt. We taxi to the runway.

'I must apologize for this further delay, but we should be off in about 5 minutes.'

The restrained smokers are now sitting with bulging eyes, pouring alcohol down themselves to neutralize their craving for the weed. We are actually taking off!!! Fortunately the whine of the engines has partially drowned the Muzak. We are up. Off goes the NO SMOKING sign, the nictine lunatic next to me is off in a cloud of smoke, and that awful job of me having to inhale some of it for him is on. I remind the hostess of her promise of a non-smoker. Luckily there is a vacant non-smoking seat in which I now take up residence. Outside is a beautiful, silent, clean, aired world. Inside the Muzak is grinding my mind to pulp.

'Hello, this is your captain speaking. Just to fill you in, we shall be flying at . . .' Here we all join in the chorus '500 mph', '. . . and we will be flying at . . .' All together! '30,000 feet. . . .'

Muzak again. I pull the call button. Sweet thing arrives.

'Can you turn off this Muzak, please? I've heard it round three times.'

'I'll speak to the chief steward.' She really doesn't understand. Why? No other passengers have ever asked for it to be turned off.

I carried out a minor psychological experiment. I asked each one of the stewardesses if they could remember any tune of the tape. No. I even asked several passengers if they remembered any. Answer. No. So will someone tell me what it's on for?

It's switched off, and a little girl in the seat behind says 'Mummy, they've switched off the don't-be-frightened-we're-not-going-to-crash-on-take-off music', and that summed it up.

Mrs Thrills's first husband as a child

McGonagall

William Topaz McGonagall. The fact that his name appears in print in 1977 in the columns of the *Observer* is in itself unique when you consider that the reason is his 'talent' as a poet. I won't go into those scholastic, dry-as-dust 'He was born on etc. and lived at etc.' literary flashbacks. I will, however, state that he was, like myself, Irish by descent. He was born before the advent of the Irishman jokes (i.e. Irishwoman to Irishman: 'Dear, I've set the alarm clock for six.' 'Why? There's only two of us.'), but if his lifestyle is anything to go by, then he might have been one on whom all the jokes were based. His family must have been dim, for at the time when all the other impoverished Irish were going to the promised land of America, *his* family went in exactly the opposite direction, Scotland. Even funnier, the Scottish were all emigrating to Northern Ireland (not any more).

But for his love affair with poetry, William McGonagall would today be a moss-covered gravestone in a Dundee graveyard. No, wrong. He would *not* be a moss-covered gravestone. No, I should have said he'd be *underneath* a moss-covered etc. etc. He is unique in the history of British literature. He has absolutely no match when it comes to what is the most appalling verse, and yet with those awful quatrains, all based on the school rhythms of five-year-old children, he unwittingly created more laughs for me than accepted humorists. I mean, what kind of mind could produce the following lines, which he wrote, among his first poems, to the Reverend G. Gilfillan of Dundee:

The first time I heard him sepak,
  'Twas in the Kinnaird Hall
Lecturing on the Garibaldi movement
  As loud as he could bawl.

My blessing on his noble form
  And on his lofty head
May all good angels guard him while living
  Thereafter when he's dead.

To add to the hysteria he added the following note to the above
poem:

PS This is the first poem I have
composed while under the divine inspiration.

He was, like all social grovellers of the day (there's still quite a few
left), inspired by Queen Victoria. He wrote innumerable verses to
the dear lady, not one of which she ever saw. Frustrated by this, he
set about a journey on foot (he was skint) from Dundee to Balmoral. He was to walk a total of 500 miles – the fact that he
undertook it is evidence that

  (a) he couldn't count,
  (b) he was an idiot, or
  (c) he was an idiot who couldn't count.

He believed that by knocking on Balmoral's portals he would be
admitted before the great Queen. During the walk he was struck by
lightning. He wrote a poem about the occasion – alas, the manuscript is lost, but I imagine it went like this:

Oh 'twas in the year of eighteen ninety-nine
  And in the month of July
I was struck by a bolt of lightning
  And I often wonder why. That seemed to come from the sky.
I was on my way to Balmoral
  To see our beloved Queen
Why then was I struck by lightning
  Before I had been seen?

83

Arriving at the Castle he got no further than the policeman's lodge, where he was told he could not see the Queen. To humour him the policeman asked McGonagall to recite some of his poetry.

'Where?' asks McGonagall.

'Just where you stand,' replied the policeman.

McGonagall was enraged, for as he records, he said, 'Nay sir, I will not. Nothing so degrading as doing it in the open air. When I give specimens (specimens?) of my abilities, it is in a theatre or hall. However if you want to hear me inside your lodge (here comes his poverty) and pay me before my performance . . .'

His offer was turned down. Before leaving he was asked how much were his book of poems (he always carried about 20 copies in his kilt). On being told 'two pence', the policeman turned him round and said 'Go home, and don't ever come 'ere again.' His whole life was like this. A poem written by him always foreshadowed a disaster.

Oh beautiful Bridge over the silvery Tay
With your numerous arches and pillars in so grand array

It immediately fell down, whereupon he rushed forward with

O beautiful Bridge over the silvery Tay
Alas I am very sorry to say . . .

To boot he was an actor, and apparently was frequently booted as an actor. He chose giant classical roles – Hamlet, Othello, Macbeth, Richard III – all in music hall. With his simple mind and mixed Irish-Scottish accent, one can't but blench at what Shakespeare must have sounded like in his hands. He must have had the same effect as sounding Reveille in a graveyard.

Strangely, I saw a lot of McGonagall in my late father, nowhere near as stupid, but himself born in 1899. The theatrical world of the day caught the minds of all young working-class people as the only way out of the morass to money and public acclaim. The music hall was fed entirely by the working class and only died with the coming of cinema, radio and ultimately television, plus the entertainment value of the motor car. Had he lived today one wonders if it could have happened for him as it did in the late nineteenth century. One wonders what his humble parents thought of him. Most certainly he revered them enough to write a 'New Temperance Poem, in Memory of My Departed Parents, who were Sober-living and God-fearing People'. It starts:

My parents were sober living, and often did pray,
For their family to abstain from intoxicating drink alway;

He then goes on for thirteen verses in which he ignores them completely.

All the family were uneducated save William and Thomas. William's handwriting in middle life shows an attempt at calligraphy, and he always added to his name 'Poet and Tragedian'. Tragedian he was, but not on stage, for all biographical notes, even his own, show that he was poor, yet he desperately attempted to rise above it. In his brief autobiography he recounts an appearance at 'Mr Giles' Theatre in Lindsay Street, Quarry'. He was to play Macbeth, but in the contract he (McGonagall) had to pay the management 'One pound in cash, which I found rather hard'. He must have been really skint because he went to his workmates at Seafield Works, took round a hat and collected the one pound. On the night the theatre was packed, no doubt by his workmates, and he received an ovation. As the theatre was combined with a beer hall one can only guess what state the audience was in by the time he came on. But! He must have had some charisma, because he repeated his performance twice more during the evening. I have the feeling it was a performance in the Florence Foster Jenkins mould with a like audience. However this was one of the few times he mentions such a success. There is another occasion – when he was singing in a pub the landlord ordered a waiter to throw a wet towel at him: 'I received the wet towel, full force, in the face.'

His last appearances were in Baron Zeiglers and Transfields Circuses. I can only imagine what the soliloquy from Hamlet must have sounded like from the middle of a ring that is being hastily cleared of what the performing elephants had left behind. In the light of human compassion he was, of course, a sad character, as they say today, a born loser, but his losses were my gain. I never pick up his book of verse without acknowledging that I have met my master. The tears really run down my cheeks with laughter. It's a cruel world that should bring about this impasse; however, in laughing at his works, I forget the failure that he was. Like the Chinese proverb says: 'When laughter is inevitable, lay back and enjoy it.'

The London–Scunthorpe Express in Bengal

Mrs Thrills on the eve of her first husband (*see* X)

X marks the victim

Is She Beautiful Or Is It Just Me?

By Worried of Finchley

I have a daughter. *I* think she's beautiful. When she was born the hospital phoned. I said: 'What is it?' And I think the doctor said: 'A mess.' I saw her for the first time the next morning through the glass panel of the delivery ward. She was so ugly – what was wrong? My wife was pretty, I was good-looking (oh yes I was). Was it the right child? Yes, it was. Blast. Long before she was born, in my teen dreaming days, I thought if I had a daughter she would be as beautiful as the sun and the moon. I would call her Laura after the bewitching water maidens the Lorelei, drawings of whom by Arthur Rackham had entranced me in my boyhood. But here I had a lump of red flesh with two little piggy eyes. We took her home. She was an angel child, very quiet, and smiled easily. Perhaps she was beautiful and I didn't see it? Yes, that was it, my Laura *was* beautiful, but I was unable to see it. So I decided that she *was* beautiful, but was it just me? When she was a few weeks old, Peter Sellers took some pictures of her.

I sent copies to all my relatives around the world. They never wrote to me again. Why, why had Peter Sellers taken pictures of her without even being asked? Was he trying to warn me? No more children? Well, I still thought she was beautiful. A year went by and Sellers came in again and took some more pictures of her. Ah! he must have had second thoughts. He'd changed his mind, he had at last realized that she was beautiful.

I sent all the relatives the photo. They wrote back and said could I stop sending them. I didn't care. The fools. . . I mean they never

88

recognized Van Gogh when he was alive. Well, they just couldn't see the beauty of Laura. I'll skip her babyhood, like she did. My Auntie always referred to Laura as 'Poor Child'. Schooldays loomed, and the fees loomed larger. I took her to the kindergarten.

The teachers looked at her and said: 'What is the little boy's name?'

I fumed inwardly and said in a cold voice: 'Laura.'

'What a strange name for a little boy.'

Was I fighting a losing battle for this natural beauty? The first Christmas panto; she must at least be a fairy. I sat in the front row, expectantly. She came on as King Herod with a stuck-on beard. I told the teacher that I didn't want my daughter to play Herod – she was a Catholic and Herod was Jewish. I took her away to a new school. So there would be no mistakes about her sex, I dressed her in a dress. She looked beautiful. She liked the school. At Christmas she was in the pantomime as King Herod. I show this photo to prove how beautiful she was at the time, or was it me?

She was very communicative. When she wanted anything she screamed. Her first word? 'Doggem'. That was the dog. The second word? 'Da-da'. So the dog came first and me second. Well, she was different. She showed a marked flair for drawing – this is her first one of me. Was I beautiful? Or was it her? Ah, what I needed to capture her true beauty was of course a professional photographer. Along came a Mr Roncoroni (*Orbit*). He had a large box camera and he took two hours and a lot of my alcohol to get ready, then he took the first formal picture of her in hat and gloves (*my clever idea*).

I took it to a model agency. This would knock their eye out! The lady looked at it and said: 'Yes? What do you want?' I explained that my daughter was a beauty and would be ideal for modelling children's clothes. She looked at me a long time. Took down all the details. She'd let us know. I'm still waiting. The world was blind, blind, blind.

She was now going to St Michael's Convent, Nether Street. The nuns! They knew beauty when they saw it. She loved it at the convent. At pantomime time she didn't end up as King Herod with

89

a beard. She ended up as Joseph with a beard. At this time I started to tell her stories and make up funny poems, like

> Today I saw a little worm
>   Wriggling on his belly
> Perhaps he'd like to come inside
>   And see what's on the telly.

She liked that. It was due to her that I continued to write children's nonsense verse. She made comments that I immortalized in verse, i.e.

> One day a little boy called Sean
> (aged four) became profound.
> He asked his dad
> If it were true
> The world was going round.
> 'Oh yes, that's true', his daddy said,
> 'It goes round night and day.'
> 'Then doesn't it get tired, Dad?'
> Young Sean was heard to say.
> His sister in the bath called out,
> 'What did dad say – what did he?'
> He said: 'The world is spinning round,'
> Said she: 'Well it's making me *giddy*.'

That was my first children's poem. When I read it to her she laughed and fell rolling on the landing carpet into the cat's food. She was lovely, or was it me???? I wrote more poems for her and she fell down laughing again, this time in the dog's bowl. I published the books. They made me rich, but I really owed it to her. I looked at my bulging bank balance and I decided that she really was beautiful, or was it my bank manager? She was now into sayings, example:

> (1) I don't want to go to school any more.
>   I've learnt enough.
> (2) I like my fat legs.

(3) SHE: 'Elephants come from the moon.'
    ME: 'How did they get here?'
    SHE: 'They fell.'

She adds two and two together and makes it five. When I say it should be four, she says: 'Then I've done it one better.' Flying in a plane over Switzerland: 'Look, someone's spilled a little town all over the floor.' She finds our cat Cinderella out in the rain. She says: 'I've brought her in to dry her.' I ask where it is. She says: 'In the oven.' At Christmas carols she says: 'You sing the melody, and I'll sing the discount.' At this stage *I* took a picture of her being beautiful.

There, there's the proof, she is definitely beautiful . . . but is it just me? She became a conservationist very young. She heard that a family called the Jenningses, who live a few doors up, had contacted the Finchley Council to kill the foxes by gassing, and she left this note at the entrance to their den.

> Dear Mr Fox or Misses,
>   Please do not be afraid of us Milligan children coming round, oh, and here is some food that we thought you might like. Did you no [*sic*] that we are friends of the Pixies and fairies and please be careful for people are trying to gas you out of your home.
>   Love
>   Laura

It broke her heart when they gassed the entire fox family to death, cubs and all.
   She was asking questions:
LAURA: 'Daddy, do you like mud?'
ME: 'No.'
LAURA: 'Why not?'
ME: 'It's dirty.'
LAURA: 'Then why do you have a garden full of it?'
   She was growing up, and that was the direction I hoped she would take. Who wants a daughter that grows sideways? Big Day

– she will look like a Princess – her first communion. David Hern, a super photographer, says he'd like to take a photo of her on that day. It was hell, she wouldn't pose, and this was all that came out of that very holy occasion.

She was becoming dress-conscious. 'Can I have a hat, Daddy?' Of course, I took her to Grace Brothers, Finchley, and she chose a thing like a flying saucer. She insisted on wearing it indoors, in bed, in the bath. She wore it for the Lord Mayor's Show. She was on my shoulders when the coach passed. Suddenly, in a loud, high-pitched voice she yelled at the Lord Mayor: 'Look at my hat.' By the grace of God he looked at her and smiled. At class, Miss Ryan asked the children what they had done at the weekend. Laura said: 'I went to London to show the Lord Major my new hat.' (Yes, Lord MAJOR.)

Now come boarding school days. Just wait till she gets among all those plain Janes. She'll be the beauty of the school. She cries at first. The school is St Mary's Abbey Convent, Mill Hill. The main house is Georgian, and preceding bishops have painted out all the nudes on the ceilings and painted over all the willies of the carved cherubim. Soon I await the arrival of the snap she has had especially taken for me in her school uniform. It arrives, and she is indeed a raving beauty.

At last. She's in the school play, in *Romeo and Juliet*. She will look radiant on that balcony, my Laura. I sit in the front row, waiting. I look at the programme.

They still think she's a man. One relief – she is voted head girl, thank God, not head boy. My friends, I would carry this story further, but it's useless. I was the only one who ever thought she was beautiful. The rest of the world saw her as an ugly duckling. Perhaps this ensuing series of photos by Grahame Stake might do the trick. Even as I write the Valerie Van Ost Agency had a preview of the photos and have signed her up as a model. Was I right? Is she beautiful? Or was it just me?

A Funny Thing Happened On The Way...

When war came to these islands in 1939 (it did come, didn't it?) morals and attitudes changed. I remember my fourteen-year-old brother Desmond saying: 'I want to live dangerously – from now on no underwear', and the condition his underwear was in put him at an advantage. We were a poor family and it was not for any perverse reason that I was wearing my mother's cast-off bloomers with collars and sleeves sewn on.

To make money I used to play in dance bands in the Brockley area. Brockley is this kind of place. If you look at the map, it's not there. The band was called the Harlem Club Band. God knows why – we were all white . . . well, off-white. Wearing a dark suit as an evening dress, and a bow tie cut out of cardboard and dyed black held on with elastic, and my mother's black silk stockings rolled down and a pair of my father's black patent tap dance shoes (the last mentioned had aluminium tips on the toes and heels that made a strange tapping sound when I walked), I could be seen playing the double bass, guitar or trumpet, all of which I did with a degree of proficiency. For these efforts I was paid 10 shillings a gig (one-night stand). A lot of money when you think that for 5½ days' labour in Spiers and Ponds' tobacco store rooms at Ludgate Circus I got 13 shillings. I had asked Mr Leigy if I could have 14 shillings. He asked why. I said because 13 was an unlucky number. 'I can soon change that', he said, and gave me 12 shillings a week.

In return for this, I used to steal about £1 worth of cigarettes a week and sell them. With this money I bought a new guitar case. It looked so good against my shabby 30-shilling guitar that often the band leader, Jim Cherry, asked me to play the case. Playing three instruments was virtuoso stuff, but having to transport all three was hell. The only transport that would allow a double bass was the tram, and this only on the front next to the driver, which meant belting around the back of the tram in the face of oncoming trams from the opposite direction, running up the side and then pleading with the driver to take it aboard, then belting back to get aboard, still carrying the trumpet and the guitar.

My talents as a musician and as a Bing Crosby-type vocalist came to the ears of Jeff Stains (I suppose it also came to his nose and his teeth as well), a very bad drummer who had cornered the market in high-class gigs among the hoi-polloi of South London's upper crust, like Masonic Dances, Hunt Balls and a lot of other important balls. These gigs paid anything up to 30 shillings – £2. In those days these fees seemed so astronomically high that when the money was pressed into the musicians' hands many of them fainted (not the hand, the whole musician). I myself never fainted. I just took all my clothes off and screamed MONEYYYYYYYYYY, then dived through a plate-glass window.

I will recount one occasion when I was booked by Jeff Stains to play a very important gig at a posh rowing club at Greenwich, so posh that they only rowed races wearing morning dress and gloves. 'Don't be late,' said Jeff. 'The President of the club is an ex-Colonel Frederick Schnockling-Thun from the Grenadier Guards who likes people to be prompt. That's how all his men got killed in World War I – the Germans always knew *exactly* when they were coming.'

Donning my imitation evening dress I clutched my three instruments and walked to the tram stop. It started to rain. One of the merry waiting passengers, seeing the double bass, said merrily: 'Can you get it under your chin?' He really was a merry fellow, and I merrily wished him BO. Eventually, through the yellow gloom, a number 74 tram ground to a halt. I immediately raced round the back up to the front, and asked the driver: 'Please, sir, can I put this with you?'

'Ha ha,' he said. 'Can you get it under your chin?'

How I laughed at him. He took it on.

I then raced round the back and as I did the tram took off. I gave chase, but burdened with the guitar and trumpet I was soon left behind. There was one chance. If a bus came by we could overtake the tram before it got to New Cross where I would have to change. Thank God, a number 356 bus arrived and I boarded it. I sat patiently peering out of the rain-slashed windows for a sign of the tram. The driver of the bus I'm sure had sleeping sickness. We were passed by numerous trams, all going slowly. My master plan was not going to work. The lady on the seat opposite said: 'Your dicky bow's melting, son.' So it was. The rain had started the dye running, and it was transferring to my shirt. I de-bussed at New Cross – no sign of the tram. I approached a tram inspector and explained: 'I left my double bass on the front of a 74 tram and it left without me.'

'And I presume you want to know how to find it.'

'You're getting the idea,' I said.

'Ah. Now.' He looked at his watch: 'That tram will be at the following stops at the following times – Old Kent Road. Stop one. 7.26. Stop two 7.31. Stop three. 7.36.'

He went on reeling off this time schedule until the tram was due at Victoria Station. By this time the tram had gone past all these stops and the time was nearly 8 o'clock. I would have to forget the base and settle for arriving on time for the sake of Colonel Frederick Schnockling-Thun. The rain was deluging down, and cold. My heavily-creamed hair now hung in wet oily rats' tails around my pale face. Every minute I was looking more and more like a cocker spaniel in the bath. In this condition I caught a number 339 tram to Greenwich. In my pocket I carried a map of the maze of streets that led to the rowing club. When I arrived at a street called appropriately Hoskins Maze, it was dark. The street lights were gas and a green glow permeated the crepuscular gloom. I took out the map. Let me rephrase that – I *wanted* to take out the map. I didn't panic because, after going through all my pockets, I knew *exactly* where the map was. It was on the mantelpiece of 53 Riseldene Road, Honor Oak Park, where I had left it. I would have to ask the way. For love nor money I could not remember the name of the rowing club. I would ask.

I asked several people. 'Sorry, I'm a stranger round here,' they all said with a note of glee. To the last one who said it I shouted back: 'You bloody well deserve to be.' Then, as I was gradually becoming the watershed for the south of England, a car – it spattered me from head to foot – of bright young giggling things accompanied by several chinless wonders drove to a halt. They debouched, and I saw they were all wearing evening dress.

'Excuse me,' I enquired politely. 'Is this a rowing club?'

'Rowing club?' said one of the chinless wonders. 'Well, if it isn't', his voice changed key to denote a joke was coming, 'it's jolly well going to be.'

This brought shrieks of laughter from the other darlings, who then entered a bow-fronted building. I saw that there was an oar outside and a sign 'Greenwich Rowing Club.' This was it. I entered a brown-panelled hall hung with photos of muscular Herberts holding boats above their heads or collapsing over their oars at the end of a race. I went to a cloakroom girl.

'Is there a dance here tonight?'

'Yes,' she deemed to say.

'I'm one of the band. Where do I go?'

She showed me to a room. Inside there was a table with a magnificent buffet with bottles of white wine. On the table was a card marked BAND. Not bad, I thought. I hung up my dripping wet raincoat and dried my bow tie by the gas fire. It was 25 past 8. No sight of the rest of the band. At 8.29 a man who must have been Colonel Frederick Schnockling-Thun entered. He was nearly 7 feet high, wearing tight evening dress, his left breast smothered in miniature medals going back as far as the Boer War.

'Where's the rest of you?' he demanded in a parade-ground voice.

'The rest of me? This [I indicated my body] is all of me.'

'The band. The rest of the band. Where are they?'

'I don't know.'

'Don't know?' he shouted. 'You *must* know!'

'Well, I know this much – they're in England.'

'Get on the stand and start playing.'

'On my *own*?'

'On your own.'

'It's impossible. The musical arrangements are for a seven-piece band.'

'Good.'

'But some of the time I don't play. There's lots of bars' rest.'

96

'Get on the stand,' he threatened.

I agreed. Carrying my trumpet and guitar, I followed him to the stage. It was the limit. The stage had been turned into an eighteenth century rowing boat sideways on, the port side facing the front of the stage.

'Sit there', he said, and pointed to the seat behind the mike. He went through the curtains and said: 'Ladies and gentlemen, the band is late in arriving, but one of them has turned up; and he is going to start playing, so take your partners for a quickstep.'

The curtains parted. Pulling the mike near me, I played the guitar and started to sing 'Honeysuckle Rose'. After I had sung six choruses I stopped, picked up my trumpet and played three choruses. I continued like this. From the floor I must have looked like a lunatic, sitting alone in the middle of a boat playing the trumpet. After several minutes I was joined by a drummer who sheepishly assembled his kit and started to play.

'Car broke down,' he said.

We went on playing, and during the next 20 minutes the rest of the band arrived. I didn't know any of them, but that was normal for a gig band. But then a *trumpet* player arrived. Strange – this gig was for one trumpet. So I asked if Jeff Stains had booked two trumpets.

'Jeff Stains?' he said, puzzled. 'No, this is Jack Wilson's band. I'm Jack Wilson. Who are you?'

I was at the wrong rowing club. I decided to phone up Jeff Stains and find out where the place was. His wife answered.

'It's at the Falcon Rowing Club, Frigate Street.' She explained as best she could where it was.

I thought the best plan was to hire a car. I used the phone and the Tudor Car Hire said: 'One will be round in three minutes, sor.'

Three minutes passed, then another and another. In fact several sets of three minutes passed.

I phoned again. 'Isn't he there, sor? He should be outside.'

I went outside with my cases. It had stopped raining. No car. I went back to phone again. Leaving my cases outside (it was very deserted and little fear of robbery, I told the car hire firm to send another car, as the first must have got lost. I went outside again. The car had arrived and in the dark driven over my trumpet case.

'I'm sorry,' said the driver. 'It was very dark, and I had to back up the street as it's a cul-de-sac. Is it insured?' he asked as I took the flattened trumpet from the case.

'No,' I said. 'It's not. Now can you take me to the Falcon Rowing Club?'

'We'll be there in a jiff', he said. And he was true to his word. We drove 30 yards, turned a corner and there it was – just 40 yards from where we'd left. I paid him 5 shillings. I was now starting to swear and going grey at the temples. There was no light showing from the Falcon Rowing Club. I banged on the doors. This must be the place. There was a poster in the window – 'Gala Dance. Jeff Stains and his band. Saturday the . . .' Today was the day before . . . Well, it had stopped raining.

Was that the end of the story? Oh no, we now come to the end of a perfect day. Fed up, I hailed a taxi. He skidded on the wet road and ran into a lamp-post. As he did, we were hit up the back by a private car. I was cut on the neck from the glass in the rear window – not badly, but as it was behind me I didn't know that. All I knew was that I was bleeding. The taxi driver cut his forehead. We were both taken to Lewisham Hospital Out-patients. Before I left, with plaster on my neck, the taxi driver said: 'The meter said one and nine up to the time of the accident.' I paid him and went out. It was raining again!

PS. If anyone doubts my story the trumpet is available for inspection, as is the scar on my neck. The cardboard tie no longer exists.

Banks

I think at last my fear of bank managers and banks as a whole is at an end. Since I was a little boy my working-class father and mother always spoke of bank managers as superior beings, and banks as citadels of respectability. My parents would blench at the thought of querying a bank statement. To go to a bank one had to dress proper, and even the *thought* of an overdraft was absolutely unspeakable – an overdraft was loss of 'respectability'. Rather than have one of a miserable *ten* shillings, my father wrote to Lloyd's asking 'permission' to close his account.

Last year I realized the truth of a bank account. Seven years ago I had earned $100 in the USA so, rather than bring it to the UK, I opened an account in an American bank whose man is 'always on the spot' (and deserves to be). $100 OK. After seven years I *asked* for a bank statement. It arrived – no letter, just the statement. It said:

	Mr S. Millington	
Credit		$93.10 cents

Surely this was wrong? I wrote; it *was* correct – (100 into 93.10 was because of 'bank charges'. Seven years, that was $1 a year bank charges.

I wrote and said: 'If I don't touch my money for another 93 years – what would I have in the bank?'

They answered '$00.00.'

99

I wrote and said: 'Supposing, when it's $00.00, I don't close the account, and I keep it on for another 10 years, what would my account look like?'

Answer: 'An overdraft of $10.00 plus $10.00 bank charges = $20.00 overdrawn.'

Banks are legalized highwaymen. Get all the bloody money you can out of them – it's them or you, mister.

Johnny Mulgrew, who used to play the double bass for Ambrose, waking up in Scunthorpe – *from an oil painting by a local artist*

About Australians

Orstrilia, or Australia, or even Australia, are all three the same country – it depends on your accent. When I was young and green and the living was easy, no one ever mentioned Australia – to me Australia had a population of 12 men, who came over to England every year to play cricket for a bowl of Ashes. From 1910 to 1930 I never heard or read the word Australia in our home.

I heard it mentioned in my class of 11-year-olds. Steward, our head boy, said to Mr Dalkeith: 'Sir, where is Australia?'

'A long way away', was all Mr Dalkeith could answer. 'And please stop asking silly questions.'

Then in Poona in 1925 I *met* an Australian. He even came into our home at 5 Climo Road, Poona. My grandfather strode in to the room and said: 'There is an Australian in the living-room. Come and see him, but don't touch him. He may have kangaroos.'

The Australian turned out to be a short, squat racehorse trainer called Tod Hewitt. 'Bloody glad ter meet yez all', he said, draining the larger part of our whisky and puffing a cigar. The swearing offended our Catholic household, but the winners he gave Grandad made this tolerable.

In 1929 His Majesty's Government moved the Milligan ménage to Rangoon to defend it against the Yellow Peril (custard and/or Chinamen). It was there that we saw Amy Johnson, Jim Mollison and other lesser lunatics trying to break the air record to Australia, which puzzled me because there wasn't one. Then I saw my *second* Australian. We all motored like fury from Rangoon .to Victoria Point just in time to see Kingsford Smith make a dodgy landing in his 'Southern Cross'. I still remember his swearing: 'Those bloody

101

ailerons are no good', he was saying as he leaped from his throbbing monster. He then repaired to the mess of the IFC, drank half a bottle of scotch, ate a sandwich and took off swearing. He was my second Australian.

I heard no more Australians (save Nellie Melba who sang without swearing), till World War II. Then I saw a whole division of them – they were marching along a North African road, swearing. They were a rugged-looking mob and I was glad they were on our side. The war finished and the Australians disappeared, swearing.

I became a writer and I met an Australian – Bill Kerr. I liked him, he liked me. He said so: 'I bloody well like you!' From him I learnt about 'Orstrilia'. 'Go there see for yourself,' he said while emptying the last of my beer. So I wrote to the ABC and said could I do a show for 'em.

They replied: 'Too bloody true – come over.' I did.

It was dawn on board the P and O ship *Arcadia*. We were an hour out from Perth when my cabin door burst open and flashlights blazed.

'Bloody beaut', said a voice. The door was crammed with reporters. 'Heave those bloody blankets off him.' :Get a few in his 'jamas.' More flashes. 'Bloody beaut, Spike, you're a good fellow.' Microphones appeared under my nose: 'How do you like Australia, Spike?'

'Bloody beaut,' I said.

'Good boy, Spike.' They left.

At Melbourne, students rushed aboard, kidnapped me, and kept me prisoner until someone paid a reward towards some children's charity. Somebody did.

'Bloody beaut,' I said.

At Sydney (dawn reporters again) the ABC invaded my cabin. By 7 I was full of iced beer and stoned. 'Bloody beaut,' I said.

My mother and father, fresh from the bush town of Woy Woy, embraced me. 'Bloody beaut, son,' they said.

I awoke many hours later in a house overlooking Bilgola Beach – it was so beautiful I thought I was dead. I was in Australia for 6 months, and that was enough to get me hooked on the country. I went surfing, shouting 'Bloody beaut' from the crest of every wave before being hurled on through the air and colliding with trees on the beach. Not once did they call me a bloody Pom – just 'you old Irish bastard'. It was radio days and on my show I had John Bluthal and Ray Barrett and I thought they were a great bunch. On the broadcasts they *were* great, but it took half a day afterwards to snip out all the 'Bloody beaut' ad libs.

So far I found them very likeable. The basic personality was British but more egalitarian and less snobbish, although the daily papers carry a snob section, i.e. 'Nora Decanera seen dining with the Governor-General Sir Aimless-Twitt at Romano's'. As to the rugged side, they had that too. You can meet people in the outback who could be living 200 years ago – rough, brutal, gentle, suspicious, child-like trust. 'There's nothing that a fight can't settle, mate.'

Yes, they're OK people. Of course when they land here they are a bit wilder than back home. They can party non-stop for 48 hours and survive.

Running parallel with this rough-and-ready image is a very fine cultural streak, and I don't suppose that many people know that at the time of the French Impressionists Australia had an identical school – just as good, sometimes better, and it didn't stop there! They've been great painters ever since. If Australia was in the Atlantic, these painters would be held in commercial awe and 'sold out' – and they're so amicable!

Tas Drysdale, one of the world's greatest living painters, is having lunch with me and my wife in the Tulip Restaurant, Sydney. 'I like you two,' he says. 'Waiter. Give us a bit of paper.' There and then he draws a magnificent sketch of an Aboriginal 'station hand' and his family, and gives it to us. Over here in the UK there is a thriving colony, increased since World War II. London taxi drivers don't like them because 'The sods don't tip', but they don't tip in Australia. However ask an Aussie for a loan of a quid and he'll give you his last.

So that's it, mate.

Someone in Scunthorpe

A Jewish dance band in Scunthorpe

GPO Gets On To Blue Phone Call Scene

It is reported that GPO psychiatrists, having investigated the obscene phone call syndrome, which is particularly heavy in cities, have discovered that these obscene calls have in fact a great therapeutic value on many lonely women. The GPO has therefore set up an organization entitled 'Obscene Phone Calls Anonymous'. A number of vile-minded men have been recruited and tested for the quality of their voice and their vocabulary of obscene words. Twenty men have already passed the test and are now training under a foul-mouthed GPO ex-sergeant-major. A catalogue of obscene phone calls is being printed. Subscribers can peruse this catalogue and choose their own particular type of telephonic perversion and they can then apply to be put on the waiting list for potential obscene phone calls. The catalogue lists some 5,000 obscenities, staring with the word 'bum' and ending up with 'Get fucked'. The calls range from 10 pence up to a full season ticket of £10. Experimental obscene phone calls were carried out when a lady in Maida Vale asked to receive a phone call at 3 o'clock in the morning from a coloured man wearing gumboots and a plastic mac, who was asked to say: 'Hello, white trash, how would you like my big hairy hand inside your knickers?' Unfortunately, as is customary with the GPO, neither phone was working, so the GPO obscenity official arrived at the door wearing wellington boots and a mac and verbally shouted through the letterbox: 'Hello, white trash, how would you like my big hairy hand inside your knickers?'

The Minister of Posts and Telecommunications said: 'This could be one of our biggest revenue-makers in the year 1971/1972. We have already received applications from 15,000 women, all in the London area. Of course, if the obscene phone calls succeed, and there is no reason why they shouldn't, we hope to network the whole country. Some of our GPO psychiatric inspectors have discovered that some women in Chelsea would like to receive obscene phone calls from Chinamen living in Hong Kong and, of course, this could lead to a great overseas market.' When asked whether public morals might be offended by this new service, the Minister gave the elusive answer: 'Tell 'em to get fucked.' Mrs Whitehouse proposes to raise the matter in Parliament, where as usual she will be told by the front benchers to 'Get fucked'.

People on board Scunthorpe Pier recovering from
Mrs Thrills's boarding house

Sex Revolution

There is something wrong with a society that asks a broken-down old roué like me, who is on a course of old men's hormone pills and walks with a stoop, to comment on the sexual revolution. At first I thought this revolution meant sexual intercourse on a revolving platform, but no, some people have the mistaken belief that a sex revolution is going on and they want to know more. Well, I've been having sexual revolutions since I was four when the heat of the Deccan sun stimulated my boyhood ardours. I was a very advanced child, which was borne out on the occasion of my fifth birthday when two dogs copulated in the front porch.

'Oh,' said my mother, making the sign of the cross, 'look at those doggies playing jockeys.'

I said: 'No, they're not. They're having it off.'

Now I didn't know what it meant but I'd heard the local soldiery comment on this dual canine gyration and I just repeated it whenever I saw the act under way. That night my father called me into the front room.

'Ha, ha, ha', he said in a flurry of flushed embarrassment, 'so you saw two dogs playing jockeys? And you thought they were having it away? Well, you must believe Mummy and Daddy when we say that lots of doggies like to play at jockeys and horses. You must believe me. You must never say they are having it away, you understand?'

I nodded in agreement and was dismissed with a pat on the head. I'm afraid that I had reason to doubt my father and mother's dictums, for a week later, on a moonlit night, I heard gasping and groaning coming from the front garden. I crept from my bed and

108

with caution approached the gasping area. There, in doggie fashion, Thumby our gardener was at work on Minnema, my ayah, her sari over her head. What fun, I thought. I awoke my father and said: 'Daddy, come quick.'

'What is it?' he said, rising from his slumbers in a nightshirt.

I beckoned him and yawning dutifully he followed me. Together we peered through the bushes at the sweating Indian couple. 'They're playing jockeys and horses, Daddy.'

It broke the back of my parents' camouflage, and whenever we saw dogs playing jockeys and horses after that my head was turned away. So you see my sexual revolution was already on in the jazz-mad twenties. It's been going on ever since, and in hard truth there has only been one sexual revolution:

> Sexual intercourse
> Came into force
> Right from the beginning
> Along with singing.

It depends on how much reference people make of it. There were ages, the Victorian being one, when they did it all the time, but never referred to it. So much so that in the great Montagu family there is a family tale (circa 1856) about when the young Earl, aged ten, was being told of his antecedents. 'Your grandmother was found under a goosebery bush, your grandfather under a strawberry bush. Your father and I were each found under a medlar tree.' To which the young Earl said: 'Doesn't anybody ever fuck in our family?'

There have been great ages of sexual liberty – it was common during the reign of Nero, for instance, for Roman ladies of high rank to bang away with young nobles after a banquet in full view of the guests. As a spectator at the time said: 'Who wants after-dinner mints when you can get this?' Any questions?

Of course there has always been a fear of sex in that it dissipates the energies. As my father said, when in a grotty bedroom in Riseldene Road, Honor Oak Park (circa 1932), he caught me playing with myself: 'You fool, Terence. Do you want all your children to be thin?' Which didn't speak well for him, because from

109

birth I had looked like a Belsen victim. The first inklings I had that I was being perverted were (a) looking through a crack in the bathroom door at my Auntie having a bath, and (b) seeing a girl at hockey with stockings that were divided from her knickers by an inch of bare pink chubby flesh. My mother wondered why I was always watching girls' hockey matches when the boys were playing football. Sex was taking an early hold on me.

At the Convent of Jesus and Mary in Poona, where I was sent at the age of six, life was a dream. 'Terry Milligan,' said the Mother Superior. 'You must stop standing under the circular staircase when the girls are coming down.' She would *never* say why, for to have said 'You are looking up the girls' knickers' would have killed her with the burden of a mammoth sin she would confess to a priest: 'Father, forgive me, I said "Knickers" today.' At home my ayah (the one who played jockeys with the gardener) started to play with me at night. My mother caught her and told her to stop it. From then on I had to do it myself, which was silly when you had servants.

My God, there was sex everywhere. Next door was a mad captain, who brought Indian women home after dark, which was rent with groans and screams through the thin adobe walls. Again my mother had the great excuse: 'He's a doctor, dear, and he's operating on sick ladies at night.' To me it sounded like jockeys and horses. The thought that my parents ever had sex never crossed my mind. I never ever saw my parents other than fully covered. When at one stage I saw them in bathing costumes on the beach at Amherst in Burma, I thought their bodies had been borrowed for the day.

My sex education happened all by chance, and my parents never breathed a word about it. Alas, it was more difficult for them. I had a dog and a pet duck and they fell in love, the duck forever trying to mount the dog. It wasn't long before we had curried duck. While this was going on, in the great life of the physical, I was being taken to the silent cinema and seeing Indian films that never allowed physical contact by touch or kiss between the two leads. It must have been frustration plus at the end of a very heavy romantic film when the hero had killed 20 would-be rapists and rescued the woman from the mouth of a royal Bengal tiger to shake hands with her. Yet the birth-rate in India was bounding up – someone, somewhere, wasn't taking any notice of the films and had invented their own ending.

Rudolph Valentino was just as puzzling to the Indians. In *The Son of the Sheik*, he steamed all over Theda Bara, placed kisses on her neck, ears, eyelids, lips, yet at the end he did nothing at all save gallop into the sunset on a horse. Perhaps the horse got it. After all, there was bestiality going on in India. In Kirkee cantonment a farm hand was caught in the act with a cow. His defence was very poor. He said he had '. . . bad eyesight, and thought it was his wife.' The Counsel for the Prosecution opened the case thus: 'My Lord, on the day of the alleged offence, my client was grazing contentedly in a field.

The judge asked if the offender had a previous record.

'No, me lud, but I should point out that the cow was cited in a previous case.'

All I'm quoting is the early childhood days in India, where, as I say, the sexual revolution was in full swing. The British in India explained away all these misdemeanours with the standard 'It's the heat, you know', and the heat certainly did have its effect. When the dreaded hot weather hit the Deccan's dusty plains, the white women of the cantonments were packed up with their children and sent to the hills. The basic and very sound reason for this was that, in early colonial days, it was discovered that any temperature over 78 degrees Fahrenheit created abnormal sexual desire in women. When the Indian Mutiny broke out the British garrison were literally caught with the pants not only down, but off. The female exodus left the field open for the attractive Indian bibbys to move in, and the sex vacuum was quickly filled. After copulating them-selves silly through the broiling summer the husbands were then faced with the return of their demanding wives from the hills, who could never understand how a husband could age 10 years, lose 3 stone in weight, go bald and become sexually impotent, all in 3 months. Again the answer was 'the sexual revolution'. In turn frustrated white wives would turn to the new intakes of pink, spotty-faced soldiers fresh from England's fair clime. Soon they too were seen to age prematurely as they went through corporals', sergeants', captains' and colonels' wives in the backs of tongas, victorias and even GS wagons.

111

The sexual revolution first touched me with the signal sergeant's daughter, who I vaguely remember trying to screw at the tender age of 7. I quite openly told my parents about it. It went something like: 'Mum, I'm not interested in comics any more.' The signal sergeant's daughter had also spoken in the same terms. It was a great sight, my father and the sergeant slugging it out one evening on the parade ground. I remember the sergeant shouting between mouthfuls of broken teeth: 'I'll teach your dirty little devil to screw my daughter', to which my father replied: 'He doesn't need teaching, he already knows', and felled the sergeant with a long, loping right.

'Why are they fighting, Mum?' I asked.

My mother evaded the obvious and said: 'They are training for World War II, dear.'

In 1929 we were posted to Rangoon, and ensconced in a large bungalow in the cantonment. The building was called Brigade House and was semi-detached. Next door was Sergeant Taylor and family, including a 7-year-old daughter and 10-year-old son. I was 11 now, and I discovered that the Burmese were really into the sexual revolution. At the Schwae Bor Pagoda, a few hundred yards from the house, Burmese dancing girls gave exhibitions of their art every evening – all very holy, but at sunset the grass verges of the lake were alive with steaming loins and contracting male buttocks.

'We'll have to move from here, dear,' said mother to father.

Dutifully he explained to the battery major that '. . . the open copulation on public land was having a bad influence on his son, who couldn't do his homework because of the distraction.' The major's answer was to have blinds fitted on the verandah.

I suppose the curse of most childhoods is the inability of most parents and teachers to give any kind of sex education in depth. In an attempt to break this stranglehold, a little while ago teachers went to the opposite end of the scale and made a film of a lady teacher masturbating. Teaching children to masturbate is almost as inanc as teaching them to breathe. I mean, it all comes naturally; we don't need *desperation* in the teaching. All you say to them is 'It's OK to do that, sonny, don't worry, you won't go blind and/or your children won't be born thin.' *If* we could induce the belief among our numbers that sex is OK and quite normal, then we wouldn't be reading tatty little postcards like 'Miss WhipLash, strict disciplinarian, BAY 3254', or 'Miss Plater, Private Masseuse using stimulating hand processes, BAY 3254.' I asked one girl who most of her clients were: 'City Business Gentlemen'. So, when you see those bowler hats behind *The Times*, homebound on the tube, he might have just come from standing naked in a cage while Miss Tittivate took her clothes off and screamed for him. All this harks back to their childhoods when sex was kept a mystery from them, and when the real thing came along it didn't make up for the sexual twilight of formative years. I suppose I was really shocked, for the first time in my life when, during the War in Italy, an American soldier told me that when he killed a German he got an erection. Now that shattered me, and the more I think about it the more I realize that the sexual revolution of later years is very timid when compared with the real sexual revolution. What I'm saying is that there is no such thing as a sexual revolution; every variation and perversion based on it has already been done.

Sex has also had *inversions*, that is, anti-sex acts that are themselves sexual. For example, George Harrison had a manor in Henley, and the nuns who had once occupied it had had trousers painted on the carved cherubs, and the penises nipped off and sandpapered down. Now this is a most sexual act, as good as actually doing it, but the thrill is inverse. Had they left the cherubs as they were, the nuns would have been normally sexed. It just goes to show the tremendous and far-reaching effects that sex can have on what are laughingly called 'Holy People'.

The best religious joke I heard was based upon what I have just written. The Pope was ailing and his doctor advised him for his health's sake to sleep with a woman. The Pope was horrified, but after, lengthy consultations with the College of Cardinals it was agreed that, for his health's sake, it should be allowed as an act of God.

'We have found three nuns, dear father, who are willing to sacrifice themselves to you, for God's sake.'

He was then handed three photographs and asked which nun he would like.

He replied: 'I'd like the one with the big tits.'

If only the story were true how much more real would religion

113

be, and the approach to sex would be far less moribund in religious circles.

I *still* don't know what people mean by sexual revolution. I mean, what's happening that hasn't happened before at some time or other? It's out in the open more, but is that a revolution? The revolution we really need is to wake up to the fact that the sex act is not love... It's *because* man cannot accept sex as a simple, pleasurable animal act that we get the fetishes which try to dress up sex, and the more we do this the more the simple act becomes lost in an atmosphere of artificial hedonism, and we find people dressed as Red Indians doing it hanging from the chandelier, or clad in transparent plastic kilts with the legs painted red. If the sex act *is* an act of love, as some claim, why the massive perversification of it into blue movies, blue post cards, gang bangs, orgies, two-way mirrors, etc. etc?

Basically I say man is where he has always been with sex ever since he left his tribal confines – that is, like a red-hot chestnut. He wants it, but it's too hot to handle, and while he's waiting for it to cool he tries something else...

It's a rum thing, this evaluation of sex. And the latent fears that it sometimes drums up in people...

During the war, a young gunner about to be married became mentally ill. It was finally discovered that he thought his sex organ was too small, and when he presented himself to the MO it was seen that nature had indeed not been very bountiful in his case. The dialogue went something like this:

Mo: 'Mmmmm, does it hurt you?'
   Gunner: 'No, sir.'
Mo: 'No pain at all?'
   Gunner: 'No.'
Mo: 'Can you pass water with it?'
   Gunner: 'Yes, sir.'
Mo: 'Then I should use it just for that.'

Not a happy ending. Again, a very tall officer went pale with fear. The cause – he was to marry the colonel's daughter, who was a petite 5 ft 2 ins against his 6 ft 7 ins. He informed the MO: 'I'm worried about our love-making with such a difference in height.'

The cheery MO assured him: 'Have no fears, you'll be able to perform quite normally on your honeymoon. Of course, you won't have anybody to talk to.' That was 30 years ago. I suppose they've sorted it out by now.

In the post-war days the search to restore pre-war romance went on. In those days one went to the cinema to see anything mildly sexy – the hottest would be Jane Russell's boobs with what was a very modest exposure; I mean, in these days of topless waitresses Miss Russell would have all the pulling power of a Mother Superior, but then it was red-hot cinema. In fact my young brother confessed to the priest that he had seen *The Outlaw* and concentrated on her boobs. And yet with the bikini revolution very little was hidden. However, old manners die hard.

I was sitting on the beach at Bournemouth talking with Col. Stanley Welch, Ind. Army Rtd. We were yarning about Indian Army days when a Junoesque female in the scantiest of bikinis wobbled past in the hot sun, shuddering like a hot jelly. The colonel followed her quivering form along the beach, then turned to me and said: 'Gad, what a trim ankle.' It was an enlightening experience for me, for I realized that what the colonel said, he meant. It was the recollection of the 'trim ankles' of his youth that turned him on, and that, and that alone, could do the trick for him. It's the story of the hatching goslings who see a human being first and ever after believe it to be their mother. That reflex was first turned on when I saw my first pornographic photo at the age of 14. The lady in the picture was starkers save for black silk stockings, and since then black silk stockings always had me following them, believing them to be my mother.

I was pretty thick about homosexuality. It had never crossed my sexual horizon until I became a driver to a colonel in Italy. One night, on returning from a binge, he put his hands up my shorts and said: 'Hello, Terence darling.'

I said: 'Take your hand off my chopper or I'll put the car in reverse.'

I was duly posted, but realized there were other ways to promotion apart from military valour or aptitude. Aware now of how near the third sex were, I realized they were in fact all around me, and most of them were very nice people, usually highly intelligent

115

and kind, which started me suspecting myself – for months after that whenever I shook hands with a bloke I wondered if I was enjoying it. So far nothing's happened.

Ah! Those golden post-war days, how innocent the sex scene really was from 1949 up to, say, 1959, when all film stars were fully clad, and kisses were from the neck up. Then, TA RAAAAAAAAAA! Out comes a film like *The Virgin Spring*, where we don't see the sex act but *just* before and *just* after, which was intimated by the camera showing our three rapists in the act of pulling their trousers up. Soooo, I thought, Mickey Mouse is in for a thrashing, and by God he was. Bit by bit the encroachment into films of the sex act and masturbation went on until we had the great New Cinema Art Form of *Deep Throat* and *Blowout*, and whether you liked it or not the box office receipts seemed to indicate that we had become a nation of dirty little devils. I myself have never ever seen any of these films because I would feel the expenditure of, say, £1.50 to watch people screwing would be a waste of money because I'm capable of doing it myself free of charge.

So it comes back to what I've been saying. There is, despite the belief that there has been a sexual revolution, a mass of steaming humans who seemed to be sexually disorientated to the tune of £1.50 per performance. The big problem is the children who are born in exactly the same mental and physical state as our predecessors 2 million years ago. They come into a world where the sex act is becoming regarded more and more as public entertainment than as procreation. I was speaking one day to one of those fey film directors who ooze sexual charisma through the seams of their velvet trousers. I said 'What's so brilliant about a close-up of a throbbing penis about to enter a steaming fanny?'

He said: 'My dear fellow,' in tones that implied that I was a grand ignoramus, 'it's the *way* it's filmed, it's the filming and the attitude that make it great and beautiful Art.'

So I suggested that, if his argument rang true, we could have a close-up on a dog's rectum as it defecated, and, providing it was brilliantly lit, and filmed by David Lean, it would be a beautiful work of art.

He didn't answer, but backed away from me much in the same way as a kosher butcher finding a slice of bacon in his sandwich, and I'm sorry to say there are plenty of these 'Fucking is Art' type directors. Just walk through London theatre land and see *Swedish Maid after Dark*, *Bodies made of Sin*, *Swedish Sex*, *Lustful Bodies*, *Secretaries of Desire*, *Two Women one Man*, *The Eager Virgins*, but cut a thousand feet from one film, insert it into another and no one knows the difference. As I say, all this, to an emerging child, must be very mystifying, in some cases disturbing, and of course those children start to see the *films* as a substitute for the sex act, and that brother is a real sexual revolution, but the wrong kind. Over to you, dear reader!

The H-Bomb

It appears that for the first time in history there exists a weapon that continues destroying long after it has destroyed itself. The resultant fall-out makes for, among other things, bone cancer and leukæmia. Those who perish in the initial blast can be counted as the fortunate.

Many voices have been raised in protest, the most significant being that tower of humanitarianism, Albert Schweitzer OM. Lord Cherwell, however, claims that 'even if the H-Bomb tests do add to some tiny extent to the number of people who suffer from bone cancer . . . this would be a small price to pay for developing a really effective deterrent which would prevent war.' Lord Cherwell obviously means well, but morally his decision is wrong, WRONG, *WRONG*. For civilization to live by stock-piling is utter fully. There *must* come a breaking-point, when the tension can only be released by using the Bomb. It needs but one man to set the whole thing off, and such men do exist: the most recent of this genus died by his own hand in a Berlin bunker. Do you think that he, even knowing that his enemies possessed the Bomb, would have refrained from using it himself? I leave you to answer that for yourselves. There will never be a shortage of men who are willing to start wars, irrespective of the outcome. That is the nature of man . . . there is *no* deterrent to man: ego eventually transcends logic. It's been the same since time immemorial.

I had been willing to accept this state of affairs as part of a man's struggle on the evolutionary path to some far-distant Utopian maturity . . . that is, until the whole picture changed, on 6 August 1945, when, at 9.15 a.m., in a moment of eternity, the first

Jack Hobbs wearing a hat
knitted in Scunthorpe

Howard Hughes swimming in Scunthorpe,
April 3rd 1951

A-Bomb killed 250,000 people – at Hiroshima. At Nagasaki, fortunately, the hilly contours allowed a bag of only 125,000 dead. To this very day 10,100 survivors of these disasters are in need of constant medical treatment. About those who survived intact the following has been discovered: (1) They are all prone to illness. (2) They have a slow recovery from illness. (3) They have a higher death rate per capita than normal. These are all *facts*, and can be corroborated.

I am very fond of the American people – I was attached to the American Fifth Army during World War II and speak with some experience: many of them were as disturbed as I was to read the news of the first A-Bomb on Hiroshima. Actually *seeing* it dropped altered the whole life of Group-Captain Cheshire VC. . . . Now, it wasn't so much the actual use of the Bomb that I deplored, but the fact that it was dropped without any warning. Argue as they may, diplomatic channels *were* open to America to inform the Japanese Government that they possessed an atomic weapon, and intended using it. Had this been done, and Japan still had insisted on continuing the war, at least the American conscience would have been clear (as clear as it could be, when dropping an A-Bomb) . . . However, that course was not taken by America.

It was this that made me put the A-Bomb second to a much more terrifying thing, the scientist. The Bomb can only kill each of us once; in this respect it is no more lethal than a Stone Age club. That, then, is the Bomb in its *true* perspective. What is the real danger, then? The danger is the trend of man's experiments. It is the direction in which the scientific mind is pointed. It is obvious that the men who invented these weapons didn't think of the aftermath, or if they did they didn't do anything about it. To them it was just doing a job of work. May I point out that the SS Butcher Squads at Buchenwald, Dachau and Auschwitz, when questioned at the Nuremberg trials, inevitably came up with the answer: 'We were just doing a job of work.'

Not for one moment do I align Sir William Penny with Julius Streicher, or Himmler, but the end product does, and will, amount to the same . . . that is, destruction of innocent women and children. This is not new in war, but then I'm not looking backwards. In refusing to manufacture atomic weapons the West German

Federation of Scientists has pointed the right way to the future. It is a brave start. Scientists working in concert could do a tremendous amount towards peaceful co-existence, but unless they do this mad desire to make bigger and bigger destructive elements (with no particular horizon, other than destruction) will go on. No longer is the warrior with the blood-stained sword a symbol of destruction. No, it's that nice Mr Jones, puffing his pipe in the laboratory – Mr Jones, who plays with his children, mows the lawn, has a pint with his pals in the pub. All in all he is a nice fella. . . but as long as he is loose – and willing to call it 'Just a job of work' – God help us all.

The only survivor from
Mrs Thrills's Christmas Dinner

Patrick Hitler dining with Mrs Thrills

Meeting Harold Macmillan

By paying a search fee of 5 shillings, and suffering the customary insults of civil servants, I was allowed to see the marriage registers of Somerset House. After 3 hours among the Ms I discovered what I had hoped. There was a marriage of my great-great-grandfather, Timothy Brian Boin Milligan, to Miss Jill *Macmillan*.

I was in! Related to the PM! For several hours, wearing a hand-made Clan Macmillan centrally-heated kilt, I stood in a queue of Macmillans outside Number 10. Finally, about dividend time, I was shown in to the great man.

'Do sit down', he said, indicating the floor. 'Be with you in a jiff', he said and proceeded to put on several Eton, two Harrow and three Lords Taverners' ties. 'Got to keep in with 'em', he yawned. 'it's the only way these days.' A GPO democratic monopoly phone rang.

'Hello, Prime Minister of England here . . . No, no, not yet, we'll wait for the Fords hoo-ha to die down first before the next one. Bye, Henry. Oh, Henry? . . . tell them to lay off any take-over bids of publishing firms, eh? There's a good boy. Bye now.'

He turned to me. 'So, you're one-tenth Macmillan?'

'Yes I am, sir.'

'We can still be friends, eh? Ha, ha, suppose you want a job?'

I nodded.

'Look, we're a bit short of speeches for the Minister of Defence. He's been slipping lately, I mean, making statements that have no *double entendre*. If you can write one that well, one that well, er well you know, one that er . . .'

'I *think* I know *exactly* what you mean, sir.'

'Good boy, you've got the right idea . . . now, do you own a pencil?'

'Outright.'

'Splendid. Here's a White Paper, fill it in.'

He shook me by the hand, gave me a travel voucher and a Macmillan's Christmas Catalogue of 'Suitable Book Presents for Members of All Parties. Free postage to our clients in USSR.'

At dawn, after the Christmas recess, Mr Harold Watkinson, Minister of Defence, read from my typewritten paper.

HANSARD REPORT OF DEFENCE SPEECH — 1961

Mr Speaker, Honourable Members . . . (here there were cries of p— off, from Opposition backbenchers). This morning, I have pleasure in giving the Government's estimate for next year's Defence Budget 1961–62. Eight hundred and forty-five million, two hundred and sixty-three hundred thousand, three hundred and forty-two pounds, eight shillings and eightpence three farthings. Postage, four and a penny.

Extras and taxi fares – nine million, three hundred and forty-nine thousand, six hundred and spon. This puts our Defence Budget up by four hundred million on last year (applause from Tory benches. At this stage Mr Crapington Plitt, Liberal MP for a tree in Berkshire, intervened).

MR CRAPINGTON PLITT: 'Does this mean we are in fact safer?'

MIN. OF DEFENCE: 'Of course, we are obviously four million pounds safer, less supertax of course.'

MR CRAPINGTON PLITT: 'Do the Russians know this?'

MIN. OF DEFENCE: 'No . . . no . . . but we will be sending them our military bank statement, and *that* ought to give them food for thought. Ha ha.'

(Light applause, tea, cakes, and scratching from Tory benches break out.)

MR FEET, MP: 'What plans are being made for our Forces at Christmas?'

MIN. OF DEFENCE: 'All is in hand, the time of goodwill will be observed, with its message of Christmas hope for mankind.'

MR FEET: 'What form will this take?'

MIN. OF DEFENCE: 'All intercontinental ballistic missiles will be festooned with fairy lights, and nuclear warheads hung with seasonal holly.'

MR SQUTTS (MP FOR A LUNATIC ASYLUM IN ALEPPO): 'But these missiles you speak of, they're not British! . . .'

MIN. OF DEFENCE: 'Ah no! but . . . *but!!* . . . their presence here puts Britain in a position of power. This great deterrent that has given us peace on earth and goodwill to all men for so long, is now on British soil . . . I . . .'

(Cries of 'American bum', and a cry of 'Let's have a little more libel' from Strangers' Gallery. A man called Randolph is asked to leave.)

MIN. OF DEFENCE: 'I admit that these bases have been built by Americans, manned by Americans, and that Americans alone have the power to decide if and when the missiles are fired, but, nevertheless and as much as thereto, the men who sweep the missiles' platforms and stand guard in the pouring rain are BRITISH!!!!'

(Ecstatic applause from the Tory benches, singing of National Anthem breaks out. Speaker restores order by distributing non-voting GMC shares.)

MR FEET (LABOUR): 'In the event of an H-bomb dropping on Aldershot, what would be the role of our troops?'

MIN. OF DEFENCE: 'The prime job of our Army is to defend England, but, should an H-bomb fall on Aldershot, the troops would be transported to safety, to say Scotland, and stand ready to defend England.'

MR MACNUTTS (LABOUR): 'Supposin' that they drop an H-bomb on Scotland . . . Ireland, Wales, and well, the lot?'

MIN. OF DEFENCE: 'The Army would be flown to the safety of Canada, and stand ready to defend England from there.'

MR FEET: 'Are you saying that it is possible for H-bombs to destroy England?'

MIN. OF DEFENCE: 'Never! There'll always be an England.'

MR FEET: 'Never mind England – what about the English people?'

MIN. OF DEFENCE: 'Oh *them*?!'

(Here the Labour backbenchers took to song with 'There'll always be a Radioactive England.' Fighting, Foot and Mouth and Kingsley Martin broke out, etc., etc.)

Visiting homosexuals

Something About Television

Write 3,000 words about television, they said. I suppose they know what they're doing. After all, all that could be said or written about television has already been written and said. I presume my article on TV will be headed 'John Squoggle our TV critic is on holiday'.

I don't think that John Logie Baird knew what he was letting the world in for when he saw that first wobbly image appear on that screen in his workshop. Most domestic inventions are easily absorbed into the house without destroying the family infrastructure, and life goes on. The vacuum cleaner, the electric iron, the fridge, the washing machine, the dishwasher, etc. all contributed to less drudgery and more leisure time, but! here was an invention that actually used and neutralized your leisure time. Read a paper – say half an hour at the most. Listen to radio? You can carry on working while you listen. But TV darkens the room, cancels conversation, keeps you chairbound for so long that people ask if you are a cripple. My children think I was born in the sitting position. My own father I caught time and time again, at 10 o'clock of a sunny morning, sitting in a room, the curtains drawn, still in his pyjamas, absorbed in the test card. I mean in my family the only words uttered at night are, 'Well, I think I'll go to bed now.'

No doubt the TV was a bombshell on family life, the results of which are only just beginning to emerge. True, Baird had invented the very first anti-social leisure machine. It caters for every stratum of human life from Cathode Gunge like *Peyton Place* to Lord Clark showing the world what a good education he had and we didn't. It can show you schoolroom sex lessons complete with pubic hairs (Remember, folks, no one is complete with their pubics) to the

Galloping Gourmet who makes it clear his knowledge is sadly lacking by putting Burgundy in a Hock glass. It devours material and screams for more.

Playwrights are severely disorientated by it. For one TV play they can get £500 to £1,000. It might take them a year at the box office to get that money, so they are, for the sake of gain, put on a literary treadmill. Had Bernard Shaw lived today, his life's entire play output would have been swallowed up by TV in six months. One wonders, in fact, are we getting rid of our Bernard Shaws and not noticing their craft in the great sea of unending TV plays? Look at me. My OBEs, etc. are long overdue. And I've had my name down for a council flat *and* an OBE for 17 years.

And the detachment with which one can view horror on the TV screen is almost uncanny. It causes maelstroms in the human breast. Heavy with food, slouched back in an armchair by a roaring fire, a fine port in your glass, perhaps a cigar, we sit thus, groaning under the weight of twentieth-century affluence and watch the sanguine horror of East Pakistan and say 'Isn't it terrible!' That of course is the right Christian statement, but as I said at the time of the Korean War, the Hungarian Uprising, Suez, famine in Bengal, earthquakes, street murders, Storyville, Pinksville, it's a sort of crucifixion in your own front room. And yet admit it – apart from saying the obvious, and sending money, the actual horror on the screen, despite its immediate proximity, fails to reach down to the level of suffering that that particular disaster demands. TV brought truth into the lounge, we recognize it, but despite billions of people seeing newsreels of the disaster at the same time, the man-made horrors continue, and by God, you know what? I think I'm getting used to it.

'What shall we watch tonight, dear, *Coronation Street* or the floods in South America?'

I mean, when a TV reporter and cameraman risk their lives to bring you the truth, just watching the result and no more seems wrong.

I myself have been wrestling with the blasted TV set for 15 years, and even though I am transfixed by it, I know it's eating me alive every night between 6 and midnight. Sometimes I stay tuned in, in case they run a test film after midnight. I go to bed and say what was the overall fascination? And the only conclusion is, it gives me POWER. Yes, POWER. Every evening I give life to hundreds of humans' mobility by flicking a knob, and watch the screen come to life. All the people on that screen are my prisoner. I can silence them. I can black them out and leave the sound. I can say aloud to them: 'What a bloody awful actor', or 'What a bloody ugly woman'. If I don't like it I can say so, I can laugh at the poisoned Hamlet dying. If I shout at Edward Heath, tell Enoch Powell he's a Fascist Bastard and I can get away with it. I can call strong, handsome men a 'lot of poofs' and come out unmarked. I can tell Muhammad Ali how to box, etc, etc. etc. The combinations are unlimited. Yes, I am a God, and I can snuff out John Wayne as he's about to hit someone. . . Click. And his image fades. If only Hitler had been given TV, World War II might not have happened. Who knows? And, of course, we have moments of immortality on the box seeing the first astronauts approaching the moon; the whole family have stayed up to see it, we even forced our four-year-old up. 'This is an historic occasion and by God you're going to watch it!'

My own professional experience of the Monster has been in the 'light entertainment' field where the rewards are most lucrative. This particular department is undoubtedly the toughest, cruellest and most financially rewarding. Light entertainment is a series of cracks into which you squeeze a programme. As I say, the money is good, but you get the least time – a week is the standard time to put a show on, and once the machinery for that show starts to grind there's no turning back. If you write in that you want an octopus, and want to cancel it half-way through, it's more likely it will turn up on the day. As the days of the week go by and mistakes and flaws show themselves, it's difficult to get them dropped, and chances are that many of them will have to go into the final programme otherwise the show would be short on time. No matter how complicated a show is, you only get one day's rehearsal with the camera team and you do the show that same night.

Because of this lack of time, writers in the main are more or less forced to write simple sets using simple plots, *Monty Python* being the only exception. Ideal shows that fit the restrictive demands of TV were *Hancock*, *Till Death*, *Here's Harry*, *Steptoe*, but all these

129

shows could have been done on radio (Hancock originated on radio, and Steptoe has since been done on sound). The test of an art form is: can it be used in another medium? *Monty Python* would be impossible to do in any other medium without radical changes; what I'm saying is that the only comedy really faithful to TV is *Monty Python*.

Referring back to complicated shows, I once wrote one for ATV. It was a very funny show – one hang-up; we never got through rehearsals with camera because we ran out of time; the show went on unrehearsed, and half-way through we had to stop. The show was scrapped, not because it wasn't funny, but because TV did not have the time (and time means money) to solve all the intricacies of the complicated script. It made me realize that TV was an imperfect medium for comedy, so I had to settle for writing simpler scripts.

For some, the pressure in light entertainment is great. It gives birth to its alcoholics, nervous breakdowns, sleepless nights; trying to write funny material in the small hours can be hell, and I've had my share of benzedrine and mental homes and the like.

TV has been cruel: it helped to close the variety theatres – comedians who had made a living with one act for 20 years were finished. One appearance on TV and that was the finish of them, but strangely enough the comics who first made it big on the box were all variety-trained – Benny Hill, Terry Thomas, Tony Hancock, Dave King, Arthur Haynes – and most of the early TV success comics were off the 'boards'.

We have almost run out of them now, but they still maintain their popularity (those that are not dead). In their place is a new type of TV creature, the actor/comic, the Bill Frazers, Warren Mitchells, Harry Corbetts, Wilfred Brambells. No stand-up acts these, but men who were equally at ease in Brecht and Shakespeare as they are at *acting* a comic character (Eric Sykes is one of the performers that doesn't fit into any of these categories, he is more an authentic droll). There are those who come off the cabaret circuit, like little Ronnie Corbett, whom I watched in cabaret clubs for many years before he got to the small screen. The current training ground for comics is the clubs.

What's it like in the admin. side of TV? Well, speaking personally, I found it a sort of *demi-monde*. When we are dealing with a show in embryo, the whole atmosphere is one of uncertainty, and everybody except the bravest of the brave will say yes to anything. As the rehearsals go on, the jokes that seemed funny on the typewriter and were funny on the first day of the rehearsal start to sound unfunny. Usually the comic (and this creature is a creature that lacks security and can only seek comfort in success) starts to say, 'I don't think this sketch is very funny' (he was in hysterics about it on the first day). Then, if the director is a sycophant he will chime in with, 'Well, *I* never thought it funny', and bit by bit they can talk themselves out of a funny sketch.

There are those comics who never laugh through the entire rehearsal and review the written material like a magistrate in office. There are those supporting actors who play minor parts and try to implement their egos by saying to the director, 'Would it be better if I said "and" instead of "if" on line three?'

Of course there's always the line 'I know a girl . . .' during the making of any light entertainment show. During the rehearsals there is silent in-fighting by the men for the most bedworthy female on the show. All the time there is this uncertainty and the question 'Will the show be a success?' That is, will it get a good press? And, alas, shows are judged by the criticisms, and if you realize that the public of the time didn't rate Van Gogh, it shows you how non-progressive the masses can be.

So, unfair as it seems, no one is secure until the press say the show is funny. And we do have TV critics who are way off-centre. For example, Maurice Wiggin praised the *Bernard Cribbins Show*, (which was a good commercial comedy), and panned *Monty Python*, which was inspired progressive comedy and possibly the funniest TV show in the world (I rate it the best). Now Maurice Wiggin is a good and fair man, but not able to judge comedy of a genre that he is not equipped to understand (writ coming: Wiggin *vs* Milligan). Fortunately the BBC have men in office like Michael Mills who have the courage of their own convictions and stick to the show of their beliefs despite adverse criticism.

Anyhow, what I was saying was that great uncertainty hangs over *every* comedy show you do, and this explains why the bars of every TV organization do a permanent roaring trade. The worse the show, the more alcohol is consumed. The conversation in these bars is very varied, but, I fear, not much of any great depth is discussed. There are those who got there first and are pissed by the time you arrive and then talk a lot of sycophantic dross. 'I saw your last show. Brilliant.' Or the lush director with 'We really must do a show together'; I know one producer, who shall remain nameless, who has said that to me every time we have met over the last 15 years. There are those directors who scream with laughter at every line at the rehearsal, especially when spoken by the comic. The comic gains courage, then the show is a flop and he asks for 'another director'. All in all the tension and ambiance of light entertainment is on the borderline.

Still, despite its neurotic tenure, it seems to attract people like a magnet. The screen has a magic quality, and people who are seen on it are treated differently. At a recent regimental reunion, a member of my battery who had never bothered to speak to me in those distant days was all over me. I realize that *I* hadn't changed, television had changed *him*! Mind you, I suppose the TV ego would be deflated if you were ignored in the street (although I would welcome it). The funniest story I heard was someone going up to Terry Thomas and saying: ' 'ere, weren't you Terry Thomas?'

I think I've written enough even if it's not 3,000 words. Make the rest up your bloody self. I had to. If not, why not watch TV.

Mrs Thrills's twenty-second husband taken just prior to his death

Groucho and Me

I didn't know he was short of money but Groucho Marx has written a book. By avoiding war, homosexuality, rape, Algeria and Lord Alanbrooke, he has reduced the book to an autobiography. This is his first book, this is my first criticism. So, come Groucho, let us journey hand in hand through this virgin territory.

GROUCHO: 'The first one's mine.'

ME: '*Touché!* Chapter one of his book is a misnomer. It is no more than a preface. It rambles on about Americana, trivia, chit chat, oblique references and a spate of name dropping i.e. I know I'm no damn William Faulkner, and/or, blah blah Marilyn Monroe, and/or, blah blah Samuel Pepys, Erskine Caldwell, Proust, Gide, and Uncle Tom Cobley and all.'

GROUCHO: 'Just wait till he turns his back. I'll call him a liar to his face.'

ME: 'Chapter two.'

GROUCHO: 'So soon?'

ME: 'The book is a meandering, easy-going committal of Groucho's recollections from early days. There is no particular chronology, he goes backwards, forwards (and sometimes sideways) in time till he reaches his present age.'

GROUCHO: 'That's a lie. I've never reached my present age. I've still got all my own teeth, hair and legs and in that order.'

ME: 'Early references deal with family troubles, brothers' antics, kindly uncles, eccentric cousins, etc., etc.'

GROUCHO: 'Another lie, we never had any relations called "etc. etc." '

ME: 'The stuff that smacks of reality is the underlying picture of a once removed Jewish *émigré* family struggling for dear life in the brick jungle of New York's East Side. Money was tight and he never forgot it.'

GROUCHO: 'Hearts and Flowers, please.'

ME: 'In retrospect he treats the period lightly, but one senses that life was tough and poverty at the shoulder, the humus that grows clowns.'

GROUCHO: 'A nice turn of phrase. If it turned on me I'd shoot it.'

ME: 'His style is unpretentious, more like a talk from an arm-chair.'

GROUCHO: 'My armchair never says a word, it's stuffed. What's your excuse?'

ME: 'My main criticism is this. Being Groucho, I think he feels it his duty to sound amusing at the expense of the autobiography. As a humorist Groucho can become a little pedestrian.'

GROUCHO: 'I resent that remark!'

ME: 'Do you deny it?'

GROUCHO: 'No, but I resent it. If you were a little pedestrian I'd run you over.'

ME: 'Some of the chapter headings amused me: "Have nothing will travel" and "Come back next Saturday with a sample of your money." At all times Groucho is immensely human.'

GROUCHO: 'First I'm a little pedestrian, now an immense human. There should be a law against inflation.'

ME: 'Through the book, his mother shows up as a driving force in his life, and though he never goes as far as saying it, he worshipped her. Father seems to have done no more than make suits that transferred his clients into Hoboken Quasimodos.'

GROUCHO: 'One of his clients *was* Quasimodo. Put that in your pipe and smoke it.'

ME: 'I never smoke Quasimodo. The book is alive with incidents of all kinds. The Jewish Wedding that is halted by, and I quote "Someone's been in the men's room and knocked off the urinal." '

GROUCHO: 'I swear it's true!'

ME: 'I've never heard of an urinal Thief.'

GROUCHO: 'Men with weak bladders will do anything.'

ME: '*Touché!*'

135

GROUCHO: 'Again?'

ME: 'The book follows a series of accepted patterns, the Marx Brothers entering Vaudeville, touring with an aged queer, being broke, being booed off, being thrown-out of, off of, run out of and stranded in, of all places "Cripple Creek", all of which is no doubt true but not unique, and I draw this observation because Groucho is a unique person.

'He dispenses homespun philosophies: "We discovered early in life that living was the only way to survival." '

GROUCHO: 'I got that from a newspaper reporter.'

ME: 'Another: "Actors are like Armies, they travel on their stomachs too." He waxes serious and takes two pages to talk of Sex and Love.'

GROUCHO: 'I admit both! We're only young once, or in Crosby's case, twice.'

ME: 'The book ambles along slowly, building up to his eventual success with the first great comic films, *Duck Soup*, *Horse Feathers*, *Night at the Opera*, *Day at the Races* and other films that became classics.'

GROUCHO: 'True, one even became Beethoven's Fifth Symphony. You are sure this is Virgin Territory?'

ME: 'About which time he admits losing a quarter-of-a-million dollars in the Wall Street Crash.'

GROUCHO: 'I was only doing thirty, officer.'

ME: 'All in all the book is a pattern of success with a few wayside tears and tragedies, laughs, high jinks and jokes; there's lots of fun in it. I think it would have benefited by being 50 pages shorter, and not so sprawling, but this is Groucho the clown writing. He admits all the shortcomings in the book, thus bypassing the critic.'

GROUCHO: 'What are you doing here?'

ME: 'It seems a bit expensive. Still, it's worth buying to find out why.'

GROUCHO: 'Amen.'

Sad/Funny Men

'Why are funny men so sad underneath?' The immediate answer is income tax. No! But seriously, folks! The question is so repeatedly asked that it has become a cliché. It suggests that comedians are more afflicted with sadness than any others. It is not so – it just shows up more on a comic, like a white shirt on a black man.

Let's have a psychological probe at my fellow funny men. I know quite a few – Harry Secombe, Roy Castle, Eric Sykes, Roy Hudd, Bob Todd, Eric Morecambe and Ernie Wise – none of whom show any signs of melancholia. Even though Eric Morecambe had major heart surgery he remained cheerful. It is worth repeating here the insensitivity of people. In this case, when Morecambe was being carried on a stretcher into Emergency with a massive heart attack, the Almoner said: 'Can I have your autograph?' So how come the question 'Why are funny men so sad underneath?'

Somehow from the past the *clown* has always been associated with tragedy – Pagliacci the heartbroken clown. Songs like 'Even though you're only make believing – laugh, clown laugh', 'Brokenhearted Clown', 'Bring on the Clowns' are indicative of public attitude. The choice of a jester/clown at the royal courts has always been for some physical deformity; a dwarf, a hunchback, etc. To the sensitive onlooker, this odious practice was hung with sadness. Again the fearfully ill-formed Quasimodo drew laughter from the crowd, and therefore invoked the reader's pity, the aura of a clown immersed in tragedy. People will always show more pity towards a comic/clown who is a depressive than to an ordinary straight actor.

I myself, in the past, have always had heavy coverage in the press whenever I've been in a psychiatric hospital, whereas when Ian Bannen, a serious actor, went into a depression it got a small mention. Again people direct the sympathy in predictable ways, i.e. a bird with a broken wing presents a sorrier spectacle than a dog with a broken leg. A bird that cannot fly is nearer to a clown who can't laugh. So the myth of the funny man and sadness is perpetuated.

There are, of course, cases that add grist to the theory. If ever the association of comics and melancholia has needed a boost, then it was in Tony Hancock's tragic life that we find it. Now humorists are divided into three categories: the droll, like Michael Bentine; the stand-up comic, like Frank Carson; and the clown, like Hancock. Now it *is* true that clowns have a tendency to morbidity and depression. Grimaldi and Grock were both known to be depressives (I myself am one – sometimes it feels like two). Hancock was the mother and father of them all. The sadness of a performer like Hancock all stems from (1) a massive ego, and (2) insecurity.

Before we go further let's look at the emotional demands on a 'funny man'. First the future is permanently unknown. If one holds a 50p in one's hand, one can enter a shop and know its value. A comic has a joke – he can enter a stage and not know the joke's value until the audience tells him. And it's not *one* joke. He has to tell 100, and each one could be still-born. The strain is enormous – hence the need for a massive ego. It doesn't end there, the next night he has to do it again, and next week, and next year – forever.

So to Hancock. Here we have a man who *needs* the plaudits of the crowd, like a junkie needs a fix; this only comes to him during an actual live performance before an audience. Immediately after such a successful occasion he is on a high, basking in the plaudits. Gradually the stimuli recede, the moment has passed. Then the reaction, the withdrawals; the euphoria goes and until he repeats the performance he is just another man. Then the doubts – *can* he do it again? One can't remain at a peak for ever. This thinking creates an inhibition, a tendency to lose judgement. It manifests itself by his ruthless dismissal of his supporting actors. They had to go – all the laughs, praise, had to be his. He was a cuckoo in the nest. First Bill Kerr was fired, then Kenneth Williams and Hattie Jacques. When the next engagement was accepted it was preceded all the way by acute depression and sleeplessness and accompanied

138

by drinking and tablets (Librium, six a day). The circumstances which existed for Hancock existed for most members of the profession – actors, singers, etc. – many of whom suffer degrees of depression, but nothing as traumatic as Hancock's.

The begetting of laughter imposes a great strain on the truly dedicated humorist, especially as it is also his livelihood – a livelihood as precarious as that of a Kalahari bushman. The clown sees for himself the effect that his gloom can create in the home, on his wife, the children. An additional burden is the nakedness of being known on television – he cannot enter a public place without being recognized, stared at, pointed at, plagued for autographs. Likewize, he is expected to appear as his TV image has projected him – a jocular buffoon, alive with jokes and smiles. This is an intolerable strain. I suffered it for 25 years, with occasions that made me want to commit murder, i.e. I had received news of my father's death in Australia, and went into a shop to buy a condolence card for my mother. The sales lady behind the counter saw me and said: 'Cheer up, it may never happen', to which I added 'It has.'

I have a feeling, being a clown myself, that if one has to mock society, for that is a clown's brief, one must observe the extremes of human behaviour from the depths to the heights. The clown is then charged with mocking it all, for all humour is based on cruelty (the misfortunes of others), but these performances have never affected me emotionally. This attitude of the public does have a depressing effect on one. So to Hancock again. By now the only survivor of the original cast was Sid James – alas, he too was heartlessly removed by Hancock. This was followed up with an act of insanity – he fired his two writers, Galton and Simpson. Ego and insecurity had transcended logic. He had got rid of everybody. There was no one else to get rid of except himself. He had committed professional suicide. Now – here's a strange dichotomy – mention Hancock's name to anyone today and it will get an immediate 'Oh, poor old Tony.' Mention his victims: his first wife, Bill Kerr, Kenneth Williams, Hattie Jacques, etc. No. It's Hancock. He was the pre-conceived image of the classic clown, he was the look-alike of Pagliacci. Beauty is in the eye of the beholder . . . so is sadness.

Mrs Thrills preparing a special menu for her next husband

Doctors

Doctors! The word strikes a cold chill – two aspirins and rum – for those wretched victims who have suffered at their hands.

As a boy in India, stricken with malaria, I suffered a sea of red-faced drunken medics who poured gallons of quinine down my throat until my eardrums nearly exploded with the high-pitched tintinnabulations the elixir produced. These men were from the Royal Army Medical Crops. They would come to my sickbed and say to my distraught mother: 'Try to keep his temperature down, it will keep the room cooler.' Despite the move from quinine to plasmaquin, and several variants, the malaria returned, which is more than the doctor did.

The plains of India are dotted with the corpses of such Army doctors, all dying of cirrhosis, which even I, at the age of nine, could diagnose by the number of empty bottles protruding from their uniform. I remember a red-faced Major – Anderson by name, doctor by profession, disaster for patients. Urgently called in the morning, he would arrive urgently at midnight, whisky fumes seeping from every pore. No smoking was allowed within 100 yards of him. He would stumble through the door, crash against the chair, fall into a heap on my bed and for some unknown reason say 'Good evening.' He would feel for my forehead and then ask searching questions like: 'What is his name?' While I babbled in a 105 degree delirium, he would say: 'How do you feel, sonny?' He treated every fever with purgatives. My bedside table was like a stopping place for clinically-induced dysentery. Castor oil, Epsom salts, sulphur, sennapods – all this on a diet of curry. The Metha, Indian untouchable, who emptied it (he was touchable before he

141

took the job) was nigh ruptured under the weight of transporting the effluent.

Another victim of Anderson was our Hindu ayah, aged 86. 'Now what', said Anderson cheerily, 'appears to be the trouble, my dear?' The trouble was this: death. Even then, in a drunken stupor, he described her condition as 'satisfactory'. After a three-year reign leaving in his wake corpses and cripples galore, it ended with him falling from a polo pony and breaking his leg. He was heard to cry 'For God's sake, someone call a doctor!' His Indian bearer, disoriented by the heat, phoned Anderson's surgery and asked for the doctor. He was told: 'He is away playing polo.' This news was conveyed to Captain Anderson, and the bearer to this day doesn't know why he was floored with a right-hand punch. To make matters worse Anderson, broken leg or not, was forced to treat the bearer who until recently was quite fit.

Anderson's replacement was another khaki lunatic, Captain Martin Parkinson. When I contracted trachoma: 'It's sand, you get a lot of it in India.' For the next four weeks, under his supervision, I washed my eyes with sterile water and Agerol and went blind. Thank god for the Hindu medic, Dr Tookrum; he diagnosed it, but the treatment! Bluestone! It nearly burnt my eyes out. I started saving for a guide dog. Fortunately somebody recommended nitrate of silver.

Mango boils. My father, Sgt Leo Milligan, grew one of these colourful affairs on the cheeks of his bottom. Mango boils, what a misnomer! It had nothing to do with mangos, no more than Dhobis itch has anything to do with Dhobis. Parkinson would prod my father's mango boil with an obstetrical finger. 'Does that hurt?' My father would answer with a scream. 'Does that scream mean yes or no?' said Parkinson. Inquiring whether father was a Catholic and getting an affirmative answer he sterilized a scalpel and made the sign of the cross on my father's bum. I thank God my father wasn't Jewish, otherwise his bum would bear a Menorah-shaped scar.

Not all doctors were as bad as Anderson or Parkinson. Many were worse. In Belgium, where rabid dogs roamed the countryside, I was bitten by a frothing mongrel. The doctor's treatment was totally unique. He shot the dog. I won't dwell on the case. He didn't. In 1880 at Kirkee, where my grandfather's Syce contracted rabies and frothed at the mouth for three days, the doctor sent him to a vet with a note to put him down.

There were some not so funny moments when my Uncle Alfred – aged six – was taken seriously ill and was being treated for tonsillitis. His sister – my mother, then 14 – stood by his bed. To help him breathe they performed a tracheotomy and he died screaming and gasping for breath. It wasn't tonsillitis. The post-mortem diagnosed typhoid.

Military comedy returned to me in World War II. My medical consisted of a doctor who had obviously been dead a month. He asked me two questions: (1) Have you got piles? (2) Any insanity in the family? I answered yes to both and was accepted A1. My first military illness was a terrible itch. I was sent to Hellingly Hospital. A purple-faced doctor/idiot stretched my scrotum two feet from my body. 'Dhobis itch,' he diagnosed. I had to paint the infected place with Gentian Violet. Wrong! Gentian Violet is *no* match for a psychosomatic rash. To a psychiatrist then: Major E. Bloor.

BLOOR: 'What's the trouble?'

MILLIGAN: 'It's an itch.'

BLOOR: 'Anywhere special?'

MILLIGAN: 'Yes, me.'

BLOOR: 'Is anything worrying you?'

MILLIGAN: 'Yes, this bloody itch!'

It was early days for psychosomatic medicine so I was given some small white tablets. They were wonderful; I slept all through the guard duty and was given 14 days detention. Thereafter I wrote on the bottle: 'These tablets give you 14 days detention.'

Sympathy wasn't the strong point of the military medics. 'D' Battery MO was Captain Bentley. It was he who, when we were ridden with crabs and not finding blue unction available, gave us all cigarette tins of raw alcohol. 'Dab it on lads,' he said cheerfully – 15 seconds, no more, saw scores of gunners clutching themselves, running at high speed in concentric circles. The night of 'The Burning Balls' is still remembered in the regiment.

Bomb happiness brought me my penultimate clash with the Royal Army Medical Corps. Dazed and doped I stood before a stone-faced psychiatrist who used audio therapy. He shouted at you: 'Listen, you *will* get better. Understand?' I grinned.

'Remember it takes 100,000 shells to kill one man.' I pointed out that I had counted 99,999 and that was where I pulled out. He threw up his hands and then wrote on my card B2. I was grateful he hadn't diagnosed it as Dhobis itch.

> One good case of malaria,
>   And one of St Vitus Dance,
> Pays for a Harley Street surgeon's
>   Vacation in the South of France.

Mrs Thrills's twenty-third
husband escaping

Mrs Thrills with her next victim

Mrs Griselda Thrills
throwing her weight on to her wooden leg
(*photo taken just prior to her arrest*)

My Wife and Cancer

In a letter I wrote to *The Sunday Times* I postulated that except in extreme circumstances I see no point in telling a person with terminal illness that they are going to die. *Doctor* magazine asked me to expand on this.

When my wife developed cancer, I of course came face to face with that part of medicine that deals with this incurable disease. It was disturbing to find, in some cases, the totally immature and almost immoral attitude *some* doctors adopted, and in some cases downright inhuman. Likewise the amateur-like biopsy. The latter case I will explain. When a tumour was removed from my wife's breast she phoned me with the joyous news 'Thank God, it's benign.' Half an hour later a second call from my wife, now in an agony of tears and reversed emotion: 'They have made a mistake, it's malignant.' It was unbelievable, especially so as, to avoid conveyor belt medicine on the National Health, I had had this done privately. I was appalled at this outrageous, amateur, non-professional conduct. The culprit, of course, has gone free and he is possibly still doing it. The breast was removed.

Now comes the waiting. Alas, secondary cancer occurred within two years. This time in the lymphatic system, and so to the expected radiation treatment. After the treatment I had an interview with a view to the doctor explaining exactly the position of my wife's health. I found that the man was incapable of facing up to the consequences of cancer. He gave me an embarrassed, sloppy, meaningless talk. 'She will be all right, she will be able to live a perfectly useful life.' It was of course all rubbish. What he should have said was: 'From past evidence in treatment based upon many years during which statistics in carcinoma have emerged, for a woman of your wife's years, with her conditions, we give her chances of survival as slight.' This information is vital to the next of kin. Even I, a layman, knew secondary cancer was round about 95% lethal. So here we have an entire case during which death was never mentioned, nor were those involved willing to give any clue or intimation appertaining to it. (Bear this in mind when we arrive at the 'You must tell them they're dying' brigade.)

So much for the immorality. Now to the cruelty. As the radiation (conventional medicine) had very little effect in regressing the disease, my wife, who had not wished to use medicine that had involved the use of animal experiments, sought help from a homeopathic healer and his wife. Of this form of medicine I have no knowledge, but in my own rationality I didn't think that it would work. However it gave my wife hope, as the homeopath told her that he had cured cancer using homeopathic medicine, one case being himself, though he stipulated at this stage there was no guarantee. With great integrity they applied treatment to my wife. It was quite obvious that these people were of the utmost dedication; likewise they didn't take any payment. However, I could see it was having no effect on the disease. I was stunned then, when in my presence the homeopath said: 'The cancer is dead.' Of course, in the light of my wife's death I know that statement to be rubbish. I point this particular incident out to show that people with the greatest integrity and intense dedication can go on a 'high' on their own chemistry, i.e. 'a self-induced trip'. Beware.

At this stage my wife did not know she was dying and showed every hope of recovery, therefore she was not in a state of mental anguish. She had a day and a night nurse, a devoted nanny, a bedside phone, a television, books, magazines, plenty of visitors. She received visits from our local Dr Thomas, who in every way was a splendid man with a good sense of humour, and he came regularly despite the fact that she was not taking conventional medicine. He still visited her on humanitarian grounds. My wife looked forward to his visits. At this point I was concerned as to what stage the cancer was at. I wrote to the doctor asking if he could pay a professional visit to her and give me an opinion. He declined to attend. I phoned him and pleaded with him to see her

147

and give me a professional opinion. I was absolutely stunned when he said, in a very spoilt child voice: 'No, I won't see her. She refused my medicine.' I wrote him a letter and I said: 'Some men take the Hippocratic Oath and then hide behind it.' In this case justice was not only blind, but also deaf. And as for his 'medicine' – could somebody name me any 'medicine' that cures cancer?

There are situations in life when a person becomes helpless; this can be divided into mentally and physically, or both. Among homo sapiens very young children present a mental and physical helplessness and this offers an opportunity for applying cruelty, knowing there can be no physical retaliation. I quote the Spartans placing babies on the roof. Child sacrifice among the primitives. Ritual clitorectomy performed on young girls. Child labour in Victorian times. Indeed, once a helpless situation presents itself to the adult world it affords an opportunity for physical or emotional exploitation, a release of sadistic instincts. The removal of hearts from live war prisoners by Aztec priests has its contemporary parallels with cruel experimental operations on war prisoners by Nazi doctors (*not* always Nazis).

Likewise a person who is dying awakes these instincts, and I think it all matures with the 'Tell them they are dying' brigade. In my wife's case it was not an isolated incident. Of the 10 nurses that attended her 8 were of the 'tell them' brigade. The first nurse:

NURSE: 'Have you told her she is dying?'
SPIKE: 'No.'
NURSE: 'Don't you think you ought to?'

Let's analyse this occasion. The nurse is not a part of my family. She knows nothing about the family. She had no knowledge of my wife's personality, nor of the infra-structure between her and me. She has been employed as a nurse, not as a consultant psychiatrist. Her job is to administer medicine and keep a log of the patient. So what motivates her to ask such a question? Likewise the second nurse:

NURSE: 'Does your wife know?'
SPIKE: 'No. I don't want her to.'
NURSE: 'Isn't that selfish?'

148

SPIKE: 'What do you mean?'

NURSE: 'Well, you are keeping the knowledge to yourself?'

SPIKE: 'When did you last have sexual intercourse?'

NURSE: 'What?'

SPIKE: 'When did you last have sexual intercourse?'

NURSE: 'That's a private matter.'

SPIKE: 'I see – don't you think it selfish keeping the knowledge to yourself?'

The amazing part of these occasions is the salient fact that the nurse is new and after only, say, 30 minutes in the house, having given no great depth of thought to the matter, makes a statement the ramifications of which are enormous. My family doctor, Dr Thomas, agreed there was no point in informing my wife of her end. Likewise when the homeopathic medicine did not ease the pain, he gave her conventional medicine that did. One day there came a locum. My wife asked him: 'Am I dying?' and he said, 'Yes, you are.'

It shows he obviously had no deep liaison with Dr Thomas and didn't ask a question of paramount importance on entering the house: 'Am I to let your wife know?' This man changed my wife's demeanour to one of depression and a great gloom set in her. There were occasions when, if she saw her daughter, Jane, she cried when she left the room. So, the 'tell them they are dying' brigade eventually got through with devastating emotional results. I still believe that basically the reason is a sadistic one. I remember identical feelings during the war when somebody was killed near to me. I always felt better that it hadn't been me.

I hope doctors and nurses in the light of what I have written will think long and hard about terminal cases when they are tempted to break the news. There might be cases where one has to tell them. Otherwise ignorance is bliss.

Acknowledgements

The Author and Publishers would like to thank the following for permission to reproduce the articles in this book:
Punch for Eccentrics, The Apology, Gratitude, Honesty, Some Like it Hot, Read All About It!, A Proverb A Week, Let Me Out!, Christmas Comes Once Too Much a Year, There and Backgammon; The *Observer* for Pull Down St Paul's!, Not Again?, McGonagall, Going, Going; *The Sunday Times* for One Man's Week; *Tribune* for The H-Bomb, Meeting Harold Macmillan, Groucho and Me; *Times Literary Supplement* for Something about Television; *Vogue* for My Day; *Club International* for Christmas Article; *Woman's Realm* for Is She Beautiful?; *Private Eye* for GPO Gets on to Blue Phone Call Scene; *Doctor* magazine for Sad/Funny Men, My Wife and Cancer; *Pulse* magazine for Doctors; and anybody else who we have been unable to trace.